BUSINESS CORRESPONDENCE

A Guide to Everyday Writing

INTERMEDIATE

Lin Lougheed

LONGMAN ON THE **WEB**

Longman.com offers online resources for teachers and students. Access our Companion Websites, our online catalog, and our local offices around the world.

Longman English Success offers online courses to give learners flexible study options. Courses cover General English, Business English, and Exam Preparation.

Visit us at **longman.com** and **englishsuccess.com**.

Longman

**Business Correspondence: A Guide to Everyday Writing,
Second Edition**

Pearson Education, 10 Bank Street, White Plains, NY 10606

Vice president, director of instructional design: Allen Ascher
Development director: Penny Laporte
Senior acquisitions editors: Marian Wassner, Virginia L. Blanford
Development editor: Andrea Bryant
Vice president, director of design and production: Rhea Banker
Executive managing editor: Linda Moser
Production manager: Ray Keating
Production editor: Sasha Kintzler
Director of manufacturing: Patrice Fraccio
Senior manufacturing buyer: David Dickey
Cover design: Pat Wosczyk
Text design: Ann France
Text composition: Preface, Inc.
Photo credits: cover, digital illustration by Marjory Dressler;
1: EyeWire Collection / Getty Images; **9:** EyeWire Collection / Getty
Images; **19:** Javier Pierini / Getty Images; **27:** EyeWire Collection /
Getty Images; **35:** EyeWire Collection / Getty Images; **43:** EyeWire
Collection / Getty Images; **51:** Javier Pierini / Getty Images;
59: EyeWire Collection / Getty Images; **67:** EyeWire Collection /
Getty Images; **75:** EyeWire Collection / Getty Images; **83:** EyeWire
Collection / Getty Images; **91:** EyeWire Collection / Getty Images;
99: EyeWire Collection / Getty Images; **109:** EyeWire Collection /
Getty Images; **121:** Monica Lau / Getty Images. All photos in the
That's Good Business boxes from PhotoDisc / Getty Images.

ISBN: 0-13-089792-2

Printed in the United States of America
09 10 11 12 13 –CRK– 13 12 11 10 09

CONTENTS

A LETTER TO YOU

PEARSON EDUCATION
ELT DIVISION
10 BANK STREET, SUITE 900
WHITE PLAINS, NY 10606-1951
TEL [914] 287-8000

August 2002

Dear Reader:

I wrote the second edition of *Business Correspondence* for you. It will help you become a successful member of an office team. You will learn how to write clear and effective letters, faxes, memos, and e-mails. You will learn common expressions and procedures used in business. You will also improve your basic English skills.

This book provides many models of the most common types of correspondence, with grammar exercises and lots of practice in preparing letters, faxes, memos, and e-mails. There is also a Reference Section, which is a handy summary of key information for business correspondence.

You may use this book with or without a teacher. All the answers are in the Answer Key on page 144. You can correct your own work and build your business skills. Good luck!

Sincerely yours,

Lin Lougheed

Lin Lougheed

TEST YOURSELF

Before you begin, see how much you know about business correspondence.

1. Label the different elements of this letter.
2. What is the format of this letter: block, semi-block, or indented? _____
3. The shaded boxes show fifteen errors. Write the correct word or punctuation above the errors.

The answers are in the Answer Key on page 144. If you need help, look at the Reference section on page 131. After you finish this book, try the test again. You will see a big improvement!

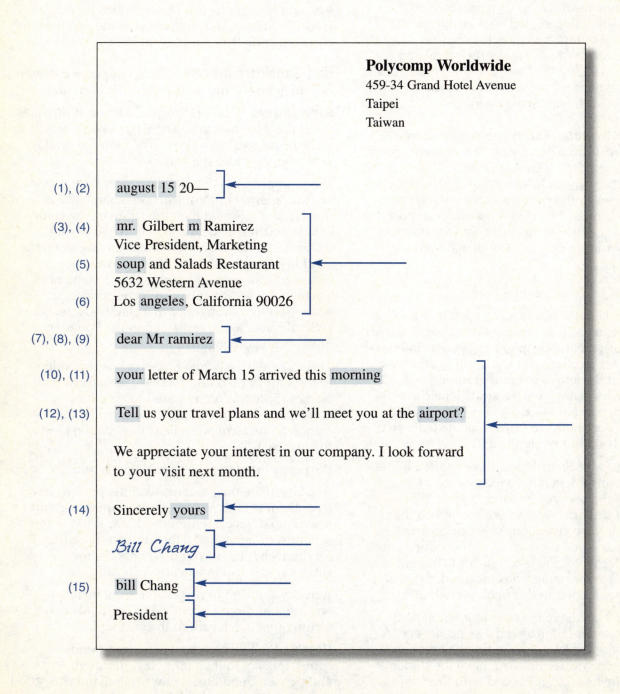

Polycomp Worldwide
459-34 Grand Hotel Avenue
Taipei
Taiwan

(1), (2)   august 15 20—

(3), (4)   mr. Gilbert m Ramirez
           Vice President, Marketing
(5)   soup and Salads Restaurant
           5632 Western Avenue
(6)   Los angeles, California 90026

(7), (8), (9)   dear Mr ramirez

(10), (11)   your letter of March 15 arrived this morning

(12), (13)   Tell us your travel plans and we'll meet you at the airport?

             We appreciate your interest in our company. I look forward
             to your visit next month.

(14)   Sincerely yours

             Bill Chang

(15)   bill Chang

             President

TO THE TEACHER

Teaching Suggestions

Learning how to write business correspondence is not as difficult as students think. Business correspondence is very formulaic. There are standard phrases and expressions that are commonly used. When students become familiar with these expressions, they will find it easy to write a business letter.

This book teaches standard formats and phrases used in letters for the most common business situations. By following the book, students will have an excellent introduction to business correspondence. You can make their experience richer by expanding the book activities. Here are some suggestions for expansion activities to enrich your students' classroom experience.

General Activities   Encourage your students to engage in real correspondence. If they have access to the Internet, have them log on to www.lougheed.com, click on Learning Center, then click Business Correspondence. Your students, along with students around the world, can post their writing. There is no better way for students to improve their writing ability than by writing.

First Day of Class

Purpose: Establish a starting point.

Activity 1: Have students write a letter in English. All students must write on the same subject. Give them a subject that they might have some interest in (asking for a college catalog, applying for a job). Then collect the letters without grading them. On the last day of class, have the students write a letter on the same subject. Return their original letters to them and have them evaluate their own progress. It should be significant.

Activity 2: Once the students have handed in the English business letter, have them write a letter in their own language on the same subject. The purpose of this activity is to see how much they know about the conventions of writing a business letter in their own language. Ask them questions about the format of the letter, such as, "Where is the date? Are the paragraphs indented?" (Look at the reference section in this book for help.)

Activity 3: Next have the class as a whole write a business letter in English on the same subject. As they compose the letter, you write the letter on the board. When you are finished, have the students compare the letter on the board with their own letters. Have them note what is the same and what is different between the letter on the board and their own letters. They can do this in pairs, small groups, or in front of the whole class.

Warm-up before Each Unit

Purpose: Let the students use previous knowledge. Provide a basis for learning.

Activity: Have the students read the unit title. Ask if anyone can explain why a person would write that kind of letter. Have students write a letter on the unit focus. Don't collect, correct, or read the letters. The students should keep them to correct during the course of the unit.

Unit-Specific Activities   Following are expansion activities for the different sections in each unit.

Getting Started   The first page of each unit provides the context for the unit. There has to be a reason to write or respond to a letter. The material on this first page provides the reason.

Tell your students that the language, format, and style in internal (interoffice) correspondence is much more informal than the language used for external correspondence. See if they can spot differences. For example, salutations are often not used in e-mail, especially within a company. Sometimes subjects are dropped from sentences. This would never happen in correspondence addressed to a stranger or to a client. (Note: Some style differences are explained in the Language Style section on page viii.)

There are generally two pieces of correspondence at the start of each unit followed by a form with blanks. Students are required to read the correspondence to complete the form. If they complete the form accurately, they understood the material.

Purpose: Provide context for letter writing.

Activity 1: Before students read the page in detail, have them skim it and make assumptions about the context. Ask questions such as: What is the sender writing about? How do you think the sender feels? How would you handle the situation/correspondence?

Activity 2: Bring in real examples of business writing and discuss them. Have students bring in writing that is relevant to the unit topic.

Models   Well-written business correspondence comes quickly to the point. It is thorough, concise, and polite. Good business writing maintains good customer relations. With each model, point out how the correspondence clarifies the issue and encourages a response.

In reality, it often takes more than two letters to resolve a problem. There is sometimes a need for further clarification. Sometimes, problems are solved on the phone and then followed up in writing. Nonetheless, these models will serve as examples of how to write clearly, concisely, and effectively.

Purpose: Establish a model.
Teach students to "get the point."

Activity 1: Have the students scan each letter to look for specific information such as date, sender, etc.

Activity 2: Have the students skim each letter to look for key words and phrases. In small groups, have them discuss the content and describe the purpose of each letter.

Activity 3: Dictate the letter to the class or have pairs of students dictate to each other.

Composing Your Message This section graphically illustrates the parts of a letter. Using this as a guide, students will easily remember the parts when they start to compose a letter.

There are many ways a writer might express an idea in a letter. The most frequent activity in this section gives students examples of these variations mixed with sentences that are inappropriate because of style or content. This is challenging because students must determine not only if the content is correct, but also if the style is appropriate. Of the three choices, two are appropriate. Those that are inappropriate because of style are identified as such in the answer key.

Purpose: Give students a formula to guide their letter writing.

Activity 1: Help students understand and learn the parts of each letter.

Activity 2: Have students look at the letters they wrote the first day of class and find the parts; rewrite if necessary.

Writing Your Message This section focuses on grammar and style. You can also go back to letters in earlier units to find examples of topics being discussed.

Grammar Practices

Purpose: Focus on common grammar found in business correspondence.

Activity 1: Have the students underline or circle the grammar point under discussion in letters throughout the chapter.

Activity 2: Have the students write a sentence similar to the ones they have marked.

Style Practices

Purpose: Focus on common stylistic devices in business correspondence.

Activity 1: Have the students rewrite letters using a different opening/complimentary close.

Activity 2: Have the students write sentences in different business contexts using the phrases and expressions used in the model letters.

Activity 3: Have the students write letters using the phrases in the Useful Language boxes.

Letter Practice 1

Purpose: Reinforce business communication vocabulary, phrases, and patterns.

Activity 1: Ask questions such as: Who wrote it? When was it written? What does the writer want done?

Activity 2: If students are familiar with the parts of speech, have them examine the letter; determine what *kind* of word could go in the blanks.

Activity 3: Have the students try to fill in the blanks without looking at the word box.

Activity 4: If students are familiar with the parts of speech, have them identify words in the box by part of speech.

Activity 5: In pairs, have the students correct and/or compare work.

Activity 6: Have the students identify the parts of the letter.

Letter Practice 2

Purpose: Guide students to reread and proof letters for possible errors.

Activity 1: Individually or in pairs, have students proofread the letter line by line.

Activity 2: Have students rewrite the letter.

Activity 3: Have students rewrite the letter with different openings and/or complimentary closes.

Activity 4: Point out grammar and/or punctuation rules.

Letter Practice 3

Purpose: Let students apply what they have learned to create their own letters.

Activity 1: Have students write the letters.

Activity 2: Have peers proofread the letters.

Words and Expressions to Know

Purpose: Provide list of relevant business vocabulary. These words are defined in the Glossary on page 139.

Purpose: Use vocabulary in context.

Activity 1: Review the unit and identify words that might be new to students in addition to those found at the end of the unit. Make a list of these words to review with the students.

Activity 2: Dictate the list; students can make assumptions about meaning and spelling, and practice proofing by correcting their words (or partner's words) against the list.

Activity 3: Have students choose one or more word(s) to use in a sentence. As a class, in groups, or in pairs, compare their words and sentences.

Activity 4: Choose words that weren't picked. Use them in sentences. Ask students to guess the meaning from context.

Activity 5: In pairs, have students ask questions. Student 1 asks, "How do you spell that word?" Student 2 spells the new word and asks, "What does that word mean?" Student 1 gives the meaning.

Activity 6: Have students pick words from the list and: 1) name words from the same word family, or 2) name words with the opposite meaning.

Language Style

This section provides further explanation on the differences between informal and formal written English. Informal English is often used between two people who work closely together or know one another very well. Formal English is used when writing to someone you don't know or don't know very well. It is also used when writing to a superior and when writing to someone for the first time.

Each unit opens with a few pieces of material, including e-mails, ads, notes, charts, and Web pages. Some of this material contains informal language that your students may not be familiar with. Below is a unit-by-unit explanation of some of this language. The alternatives given show the more formal way to say the same thing.

Unit 1   Ads (p. 1)

Informal (ad)   A college degree is a must.
Formal   A college degree is an essential requirement.

The use of *must* is idiomatic. It is often used in ads or conversations. It is generally not used in formal written English.

Informal (ad)   E-mail résumé to . . .
Formal   Please e-mail your résumé to . . .

In ads, words are often deleted to conserve space. The word *résumé* comes from the French. It can also be written without the accent marks: *resume*.

Informal (ad)   The admin. asst. will . . .
Formal   The administrative assistant will . . .

Administrative assistant is shortened to *admin. asst.* This is common in advertisements, where space is at a premium, or in conversations. Similarly the administrative department in a company is often referred to as the *Admin Department* or simply *admin* (*I'll be in admin all morning.*)

Unit 2   Interoffice e-mail (p. 9)

Informal   Thanks for sending out the acknowledgment e-mails.
Formal   I would like to thank you for sending the e-mails to the job applicants acknowledging the receipt of their applications.

Unit 3   Interoffice e-mails (p. 19)

Informal   I got a brochure.
Formal   I received a brochure.

Informal   See if they can . . .
Formal   If you have time, would you please call them and ask if they could . . .

Informal   Lunch is no problem.
Formal   They would be pleased to cater a lunch.

Unit 4   Interoffice memos (p. 27)

Informal   They haven't gotten back to me.
Formal   They haven't returned my call to tell me what they want.

Informal   Could you follow up?
Formal   Would you be able to contact them and determine what they need?

Informal   . . . a buffet lunch would be OK.
Formal   . . . a buffet lunch would be fine.

Informal   Any other problems? Let me know.
Formal   If you have any other problems you would like to discuss, please let me know.

Unit 5   Note from the Desk of M. Simpson (p. 35)

The verb *order* in the last sentence is not followed by a direct object. In informal interoffice correspondence, the writer may not think it necessary to write *order them today.* The object *them* is understood.

Unit 6   E-mail (p. 43)

Informal They're going to be a week behind schedule.
Formal They will be a week behind schedule.

Informal Please call customers who ordered this chip set.
Formal Would you please call those customers who ordered this chip set?

There is no rule that governs when you can or can't delete an article or demonstrative pronoun like *those*. It is safer to use the formal form.

Informal Ask if we can substitute ACB 5/x/233.
Formal Would you please ask if it would be possible to substitute ACB 5/x/233 for the Intex 440SX chip?

Informal We have those chip sets on hand.
Formal We currently have those chip sets in stock.

Unit 7   Interoffice e-mail (p. 51)

Informal Could you check it out?
Formal Would you please research the information?

Unit 8   Interoffice e-mails (p. 59)

Most of the language used in these e-mails would be appropriate for any type of business communications. In more formal correspondence, the abbreviations *reps* and *info* would be spelled out: *representatives* and *information*. Note these two abbreviations are used as words; they are not followed by periods.

Unit 9   Interoffice e-mails (p. 67)

The e-mail begins with "Mark, . . ." as if H. Park were actually talking to Mark. E-mails can be very conversational. The e-mail continues with a rhetorical question: *Doesn't anyone read our POs?* When you ask a rhetorical question, you don't expect an answer.

Mark replies that *MarvelSoft has real problems.* In this instance, *real* means "a lot of" problems or "very serious" problems.

Unit 10   Interoffice e-mails (p. 75)

Informal Best Ads Online returned 4 manuals—old editions.
Formal Best Ads Online returned four manuals because the manuals were out-of-date.

Informal Empress Trading sent back the accounting package—damaged CD.
Formal Empress Trading company returned the accounting package because the CD was damaged.

Ms. Gerard lists the reasons for the return using a dash. This is an informal, conversational style.

Informal I'll check into it.
Formal I'll investigate the problem.

Ms. Gerard asks many questions: *Why are we getting so many returns? What's going on here? Who's filling these orders?* These are not rhetorical questions. She expects answers. Sometimes it is hard to tell when a question is rhetorical, especially in e-mails.

Mr. Weiss begins his response by saying: *It seems our customer service . . .* By saying, *It seems*, he puts the responsibility for the problem on someone other than himself.

Unit 11   Interoffice e-mails (p. 83)

Informal Check receivables.
Formal Would you please look over the list of accounts receivable?

Informal See if we received payment from Gornan Industries.
Formal Would you please determine if we received payment from Gornan Industries?

Informal Have other reminders gone out?
Formal Would you tell me if other reminder letters have been sent?

Formal What next?
Informal Please tell me if there is anything else you would like me to do.

The verb *is* is dropped in *What next?* This is written in a conversational style.

S. Caffey uses the plural possessive (*their*) referring to a company Alliance. This acknowledges the fact that there are people working in the company who do the work. A company may be singular, but the employees are plural. The writer could say, *For their May invoice, For Alliance's May invoice,* or *For its May invoice.*

Unit 12   Interoffice e-mails (p. 91)

Tone 1 Do I have authorization to pay these invoices?
Tone 2 Would you please authorize me to pay these invoices?

These sentences illustrate differences in tone and intent rather than formality. The writer doesn't have authorization to pay invoices without permission from a superior. In the first sentence, the writer uses the pronoun *I* which makes it seem as if he has some power. In the second sentence, it is clearly the superior, *you*, with the power.

Informal Wait for now.

Formal Please don't pay the invoice until further notice.

A stop-payment order is also called a stop-check order. A check lost in the mail could be found by someone and cashed. To avoid this potential problem, the writer of the check can call the bank and place a stop-payment order on the check, which means that nobody can cash the check. There is a bank fee for this service.

Unit 13 Interoffice e-mails (p. 99).

Informal Also, Ming-Tang is going to two of our offices in China next week. You should e-mail our branch managers in Beijing and Shanghai to introduce him.

Formal You should also write an e-mail to our branch managers in Beijing and Shanghai to introduce Ming-Tang who is going to China next week.

The use of *also* at the beginning of the sentence is very conversational. It introduces a new thought that is similar to the one just mentioned—writing letters. In formal written English, the adverb *also* is placed near the similar action.

Informal I'm way ahead of you.

Formal I have already thought about that and have put a plan into action.

Informal I'll do Michelle Fung's announcement tomorrow.

Formal I will write Michelle Fung's announcement letter tomorrow.

Unit 14 Interoffice e-mails (p. 109).

Informal Also, don't forget . . .

Formal There is one more task for you to remember to do.

See the note on *also* in Unit 13 above.

Informal No problem.

Formal I have taken care of the tasks already.

Informal The addresses were pulled on Jan. 3.

Formal The addresses were retrieved from the database on January 3.

Unit 15 Interoffice e-mails (p. 121)

Informal Would you draft a thank-you letter to May Wing for referring us to Xenest?

Formal Would you please draft a letter to May Wing thanking her for referring us to Xenest?

Informal Lisa,

Formal Dear Lisa,

Remember in interoffice communication between colleagues, you can address the person as if you were talking in person or you can omit the salutation all together.

Informal Sorry to hear about Jeong-tae's father.

Formal I am sorry to hear the news about Jeong-tae's father.

Informal When you get a chance,

Formal If you have the opportunity,

Informal BTW,

Formal By the way,

BTW is generally used in e-mails only.

In *Also, the father of Park Jeong-tae, CEO of PacMoon.com, passed away yesterday*, the writer uses *also* to mean another task.

The writer uses the conditional tense *Would you draft . . .* to be polite. Adding the word *please* would make the request even more polite.

I'm at a loss for words means "It is difficult for me to compose a letter of condolence."

Speaking of . . . means "While we are discussing the matter . . . "

Acknowledgments The author gratefully acknowledges the efforts of those whose insights and hard work have made this book what it is. Comments from the following reviewers provided invaluable guidance:

Susan Caesar, Korea University• **J. Lazaro da Silva,** private instructor, Brazil • **Paul H. Faust,** Tezukayama College, Nara, Japan • **Haeyoung Han,** Halla Institute of Technology, Korea • **Yasuko Hashimoto,** Yamanashi Eiwa Junior Women's College, Japan • **Samantha Jones,** El Centro College, Dallas, Texas • **Conceicao Maria Ferreira Sarmento Rito Lange,** private instructor, Brazil • **Grace Jih-Jen Liou,** National Kaoshiung Institute of Technology, Taiwan • **Leonard Lundmark,** Wakayama University, Japan • **Mark Zeid,** Hiroshima College of Foreign Languages, Japan

Many individuals at Pearson Education/Longman ELT were also instrumental in creating this book, including: Marian Wassner, Senior Acquisitions Editor; Andrea Bryant, Development Editor; Ginny Blanford, Senior Acquisitions Editor; and Sasha Kintzler, Production Editor.

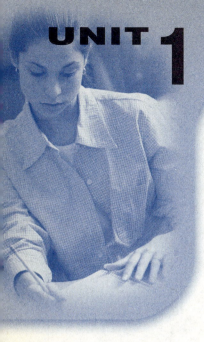

UNIT 1 Writing a Cover Letter

When you apply for a job, you need to send a résumé and a cover letter. A résumé is a written list that describes your education and the jobs you have had. (A sample résumé is in the reference section of this book on page 134.) A cover letter introduces you to the person who is hiring for the job.

Before you write the cover letter, you need information about the job, especially the qualifications needed. The best place to find this information is in the advertisement where you learned about the job.

GETTING STARTED

1. Read the two job advertisements. Pay attention to the qualifications needed.
2. Complete the Job Requirements Chart. Write a check (✔) if the job advertisement asks for the requirement.
3. Write a check (✔) if *your* skills match the requirement.

Address: @ http://www.netlives.com   GO

NetLives

The ADMINISTRATIVE ASSISTANT will work with the general manager. The individual will manage schedules, order supplies, prepare expense reports, and perform general word processing. The admin. asst. will be responsible for mailings, faxes, photocopying, and filing.

A high school degree and a minimum of 2 years of experience are required.

NetLives offers a fun, dynamic, and innovative work environment.

Contact Information
Maria Sanchez
Human Resource Specialist
msanchez@netlives.com

NetLives Ltd.
632 Garrison Road
Cambridge CB4 1HD
Tel: 1223 334566
Fax: 1223 534987

About NetLives

Administrative Assistant

A local Internet service provider has a full-time position available for an administrative assistant. This individual will perform general administrative duties. Candidates must be familiar with word processing programs. Successful candidates must also have excellent communication skills. A college degree is a must. Salary: $25,000 to $35,000 per year.
E-mail résumé to resumespptsrvc@acaison.net.

	Web site Ad	Newspaper Ad	Requirement	Your Skills
JOB REQUIREMENTS CHART				
(1)			Will perform general administrative duties such as photocopying and filing.	
(2)			Will have a college degree.	
(3)			Must be familiar with word processing programs.	
(4)			Will have at least 2 years of experience as an administrative assistant.	
(5)			Must have excellent communication skills.	

Model Cover Letter

Look at the different elements of a cover letter.

Return Address
This is your personal letterhead. Put your contact information here.

Michele Peters
45 Agate Road
London NW6 0AH
Tel: 208 847 9746
Fax: 208 774 8094
E-mail: mpeters@londonmail.com

Date

March 1, 20—

Inside Address
Write a cover letter to a specific person, if possible.

Maria Sanchez
Human Resource Specialist
NetLives Ltd.
632 Garrison Road
Cambridge CB4 1HD

Salutation
Use a colon after the name.

Dear Ms. Sanchez:

Opening
Tell (1) that you are applying for a job and (2) the source of your information.

I read about a job opening for an administrative assistant on the NetLives Web site.

Focus
Tell why you are suited for the job.

I am a recent graduate of EMP Secretarial School, and I was in the top of my class. I am looking for a challenging work environment like that at NetLives.

Action
Tell what you plan to do.

I will call you next Monday to discuss my enclosed résumé.

Closing
Be positive.

I look forward to meeting with you soon.

Complimentary Close

Sincerely yours,

Signature
Sign your name.

Michele Peters

Typed Name

Michele Peters

Enclosure
Add this if you are sending something with the letter.

Enclosure

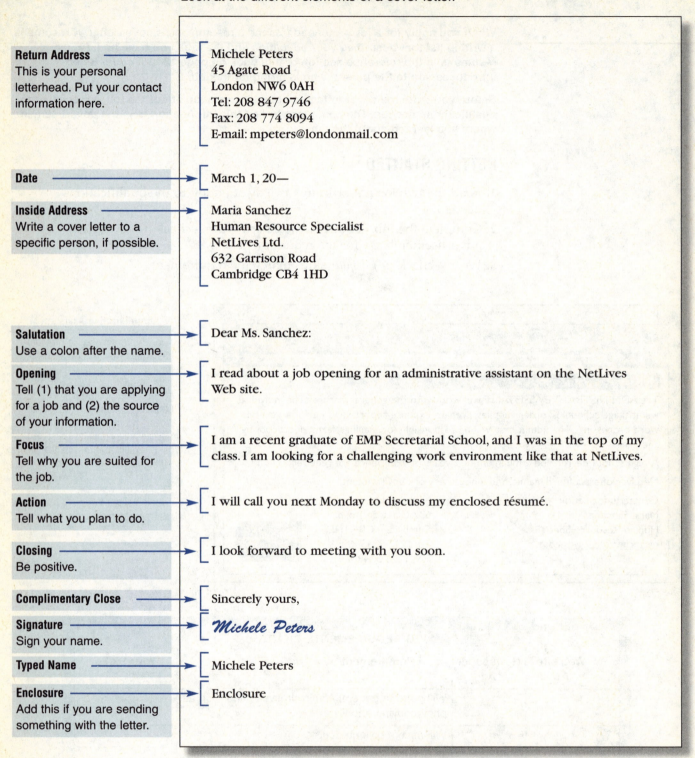

Useful Language

I read about a job opening for _____ .

I will call you _____ .

I look forward to meeting you.

The body of a cover letter generally has four parts.

Part	Content	Example
Opening	Tell (1) that you are applying for a job and (2) the source of your information.	I read about a job opening for an administrative assistant on the NetLives Web site.
Focus	Tell why you are suited for the job.	I am a recent graduate of EMP Secretarial School, and I was in the top of my class. I am looking for a challenging work environment like that at NetLives.
Action	Tell what you plan to do.	I will call you next Monday to discuss my enclosed résumé.
Closing	Be positive.	I look forward to meeting with you soon.

Practice 1

Circle the letter of the sentence that is most similar to the sentence in the Model Cover Letter on page 2.

1. **Opening**
   a. I am applying for the position of administrative assistant.
   b. I need a job.
   c. I saw your advertisement for an administrative assistant in the November 14 *International Herald Tribune*.

2. **Focus**
   a. My work experience matches your requirements. I worked as an administrative assistant for two years.
   b. I'm a quick learner. I've never worked before.
   c. I have the skills required. I am familiar with word processing programs.

3. **Action**
   a. I will contact you early next week.
   b. I will call you on Tuesday morning to discuss the position.
   c. I'll be at home if you need me.

4. **Closing**
   a. Looks good, right?
   b. I look forward to working with NetLives.
   c. I look forward to talking to you next week.

That's Good Business!

Look at the NetLives advertisement on page 1. Ads often use abbreviations, such as *admin. asst.* for *administrative assistant*. Ads also use numerals (such as *2*) instead of spelling out words (*two*). Using abbreviations in ads saves space and money. Do not use abbreviations like this in a business letter.

Salutation

That's Good Business!

You want to make a good first impression with your cover letter. You want your letter to stand out from the others. Be positive. Let the employer know how you are suited for the job. Follow up your letter with a phone call.

- Write to a specific person. Before you write, try to find out the name (and gender) of the person you are writing to. You can call the company or check their Web site.

  Dear Ms. Maroon:

  Dear Mr. Ping:

- If you don't know the gender, use the person's full name or initial.

  Dear Lin Croft:

  Dear D. Maxon:

- If you don't know the name, use the person's title.

  Dear Human Resource Specialist:

  Dear Recruiter:

- If you know only the address, use a generic salutation.

  Good morning:

Practice 2   Write the salutation for a cover letter for the following jobs. Don't forget the colon.

	Position	Source	Contact
1.	Customer Service Representative	May 13 *Herald Tribune*	M. Pollard
2.	Administrative Assistant	A-Way.com Web site	recruiter@a-way.com
3.	Receptionist	IronGate.com Web site	Jane Bowles
4.	Executive Assistant	Word-of-mouth	Chee Yu

1. *Dear M. Pollard:*   3. _____

2. _____   4. _____

Opening

In the opening of a cover letter, tell the reader two things: (1) what job you are applying for and (2) the source of your information.

Practice 3   Complete these opening sentences for cover letters for the jobs in Practice 2. Use the prepositions *about*, *for*, *in*, and *on*. Some prepositions will be used more than one time.

1. I saw your advertisement _____ a customer service representative _____ the May 13 *Herald Tribune.*

2. I am applying _____ the position of administrative assistant announced _____ the A-Way.com Web site.

3. _____ the IronGate.com Web site, I read _____ an opening _____ a receptionist.

4. Your colleague, Jannie Qin, told me _____ the executive assistant opening.

Focus

The body of a cover letter focuses on your skills. Briefly describe why you are suited for the job. Tell the reader how your skills match the job requirements.

Practice 4 Look at the skills you checked for the administrative assistant positions on page 1. Write sentences that describe your experience and skills and explain how you are suited for the job.

1. My work experience matches your requirements.

   I worked as an administrative assistant for two years.

2. My qualifications fit your needs. _____

3. My skills match the job requirements. _____

4. I have the skills required. _____

5. I meet the job requirements. _____

Action

Follow-up is very important. After you send a cover letter and résumé, contact the employer. In your cover letter, give either a general or a specific time that you will call or e-mail.

   General   I will call you *early next week.*
   Specific   I will call you *next Monday.*

Practice 5 Write *G* if the action has a general time or *S* if the action has a specific time.

1. _____ I will contact you early next week.

2. _____ I will call you on Tuesday morning to make an appointment.

3. _____ I will e-mail you next week to arrange an interview.

4. _____ On Friday, I will call your assistant to set up an interview.

5. _____ I will telephone you tomorrow to answer any questions you have.

Closing

In the closing, be sure to thank the reader for looking at your letter. Be positive. Mention a future conversation or meeting.

Practice 6 Rewrite these sentences using the expression *I look forward to* [+ *-ing* verb].

1. I want to work with IronGate.

   I look forward to working with IronGate.

2. I'd like to talk to you next week. _____

3. I'd like to meet with you. _____

4. I probably should discuss my interest in A-Way with you.

   _____

5. I hope I can contribute to your team. _____

Complete the sentences in this letter. Use the job advertisement and the words below.

Changi News

July 2, 20—

File clerk wanted. Must have high school degree. Send résumé to Mr. Paul Rook, Human Resource Director, Island International Airport, Singapore 659589.

---

applying   forward   part-time   Resource
enclosed   interview   position   Sincerely

Well SAID

In this letter, the writer uses *2nd* in the date *July 2nd*. This is called an *ordinal number*. The number *2* alone is a *cardinal number*.

You can use either type of number in the body a letter, but in the date at the top always use a cardinal number (*July 17*).

Be consistent in your letter. If you use an ordinal number in one sentence, use ordinal numbers in the other sentences.

(Write your address here.) _____
_____
_____

July 17, 20—

Mr. Paul Rook

Human (1) _____ Director

Island International Airport

Singapore 659589

Dear Mr. Rook:

I am (2) _____ for the position of file clerk that was advertised in the July 2nd *Changi News*.

I worked as a (3) _____ file clerk after school for three years. Now I am looking for a full-time position. I have (4) _____ my résumé, and I would like to schedule an (5) _____ .
I will call you early next week to follow up on my application. I look (6) _____ to discussing this (7) _____ with you.

(8) _____ yours,

_____ *(Write your name here.)*
_____ *(Print your name here.)*

Enclosure

That's Good Business!

When you send material, such as a résumé, with a letter, add the word *Enclosure* at the end of the letter. You can write what is enclosed (*Enclosure: Résumé*), but it is not necessary.

Liu Shia saw this job advertisement on a Web site and answered it. The shaded boxes show ten places where she made errors. Write the correct word or punctuation above the errors. The first one is done for you.

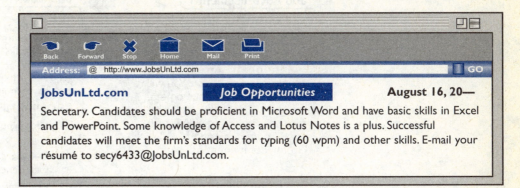

JobsUnLtd.com   **Job Opportunities**   August 16, 20—

Secretary. Candidates should be proficient in Microsoft Word and have basic skills in Excel and PowerPoint. Some knowledge of Access and Lotus Notes is a plus. Successful candidates will meet the firm's standards for typing (60 wpm) and other skills. E-mail your résumé to secy6433@JobsUnLtd.com.

To: secy6433@JobsUnLtd.com

(1) **Subject:** Secretarial Positioning   *Position*

(2) Dear Recruiter,

(3), (4) I am responding for the secretarial vacancy posted on August 16 in your Web site.

(5) I have been an executive secretary since five years. I also have trained other

(6), (7) secretaryes how to use word processing and accounting software   I type over

90 wpm, and I am very organized. I have attached my résumé to this e-mail.

(8), (9) I will e-mail you next week to follow up on my apply. I look forward to hear from

you soon.

(10) Sincere yours,

Liu Shia

On a separate piece of paper, write responses to one of the following job advertisements.

Job Advertisement 1

Receptionist

Entry-level position for receptionist in dynamic construction company. You will enter data, greet customers, maintain database, and type memos. Prefer individual with good communication skills. Great compensation. Apply today!

Job Experience
Filing, General Office, Data Entry

Additional Information
Salary: $9.00 to $12.00 per hour

Contact Information
Account Executive, myan@constructnow.com

Job Advertisement 2

Web Discount Corporation of Barcelona, Spain, seeks full-time Client Services Coordinator. Responsibilities include greeting clients, answering telephones, and performing other clerical functions.

REQUIREMENTS:

1. High school diploma and/or business college program
2. 2–4 years of clerical or administrative experience
3. Excellent organizational skills
4. Typing speed of 30 wpm
5. Word processing and database experience
6. Good communication skills

If you would like to work in an exciting environment, fax or e-mail your résumé to:
Pablo Cavero
Fax: 93 412 1044
E-mail: pcavero@webdiscount.org.es

Well SAID

Most people use one of two styles for writing dates.

U.S. style   March 1, 20—
Non-U.S. style   1 March 20—

This book uses U.S. style. Of course, you should use your country's style when you write letters.

The month in a date is usually written out in a letter. In business forms, the month can be written as a number. Be sure it is clear which number is the month. In a letter, it may be unclear to use all numbers, especially if the writer and the reader use different styles.

U.S. style   03/01/03 is March 1, 2003
Non-U.S. style   03/01/03 is 3 January 2003

Words and Expressions to Know

Look at this list of words and expressions that were used in the unit. Their definitions are in the glossary at the end of the book.

attach	colleague	follow up	post	requirement
candidate	follow-up	opening	proficient	vacancy

UNIT 2

Replying to a Job Applicant

A résumé and cover letter make up a job application. When you receive a job application, first send a letter acknowledging that you received it. After you read the job application, decide whether to interview or reject the applicant. Send all applicants either an interview letter or a rejection letter.

Before you reply to job applicants, you must evaluate their skills. Compare the skills they listed in their résumé and cover letter with the requirements you listed in your job advertisement.

GETTING STARTED

1. Read the e-mail from a human resource specialist to her assistant. She discusses replying to job applicants. The assistant will send interview letters to applicants who meet four or all five of the requirements.
2. Think about your skills. Do you meet the requirements?
3. Complete the Applicant Evaluation Chart. Write *I* for *interview* or *R* for *reject* for each applicant and yourself in the bottom row.

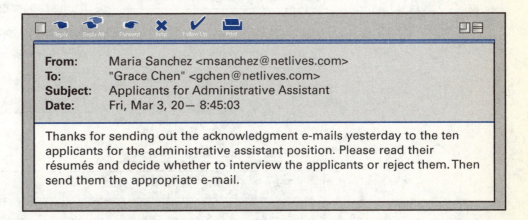

	From:	Maria Sanchez <msanchez@netlives.com>
	To:	"Grace Chen" <gchen@netlives.com>
	Subject:	Applicants for Administrative Assistant
	Date:	Fri, Mar 3, 20— 8:45:03

Thanks for sending out the acknowledgment e-mails yesterday to the ten applicants for the administrative assistant position. Please read their résumés and decide whether to interview the applicants or reject them. Then send them the appropriate e-mail.

y = applicant has the skill
y* = applicant has the skill and is a very good candidate
n = applicant doesn't have the skill
? = résumé doesn't say if applicant has the skill

APPLICANT EVALUATION CHART

Applicants										Requirement	Your Skills
(1)	(2)	(3)	(4)	(5)	(6)	(7)	(8)	(9)	(10)		
y	y	n	y	y	y	?	y	y	n	Has a high school degree or equivalent.	
y*	n	?	n	y	y	?	n	y	?	Has scheduling and ordering experience.	
y	y*	n	n	y	?	y	y	y	y*	Is familiar with word processing programs.	
y	?	n	?	y	n	n	y	y*	n	Has at least two years of experience as an admin. asst.	
y*	y	?	?	y	n	y	y	?	y	Is organized and detail-oriented.	
										Interview (I) or Reject (R)	

9

Model E-Mails: Replying to Job Applicants

Look at the different elements of e-mails replying to job applicants.

Reply 1: Acknowledging Receipt of an Application

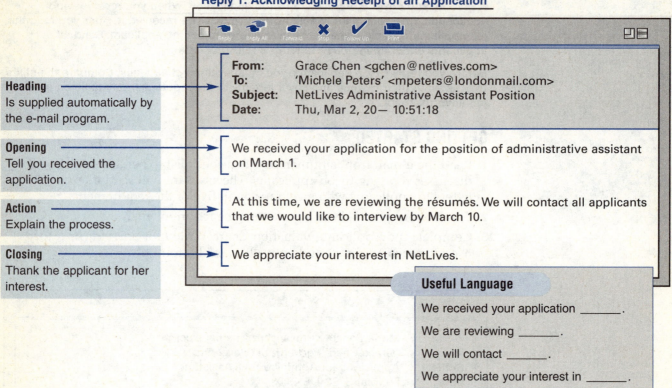

Heading
Is supplied automatically by the e-mail program.

Opening
Tell you received the application.

Action
Explain the process.

Closing
Thank the applicant for her interest.

From: Grace Chen <gchen@netlives.com>
To: 'Michele Peters' <mpeters@londonmail.com>
Subject: NetLives Administrative Assistant Position
Date: Thu, Mar 2, 20— 10:51:18

We received your application for the position of administrative assistant on March 1.

At this time, we are reviewing the résumés. We will contact all applicants that we would like to interview by March 10.

We appreciate your interest in NetLives.

Useful Language

We received your application _____ .

We are reviewing _____ .

We will contact _____ .

We appreciate your interest in _____ .

Reply 2: Requesting an Interview

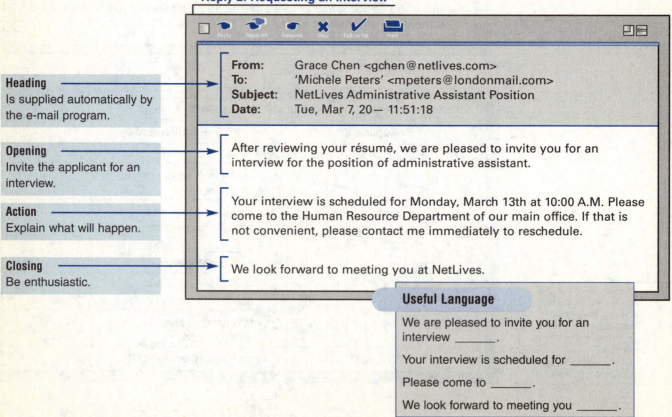

Heading
Is supplied automatically by the e-mail program.

Opening
Invite the applicant for an interview.

Action
Explain what will happen.

Closing
Be enthusiastic.

From: Grace Chen <gchen@netlives.com>
To: 'Michele Peters' <mpeters@londonmail.com>
Subject: NetLives Administrative Assistant Position
Date: Tue, Mar 7, 20— 11:51:18

After reviewing your résumé, we are pleased to invite you for an interview for the position of administrative assistant.

Your interview is scheduled for Monday, March 13th at 10:00 A.M. Please come to the Human Resource Department of our main office. If that is not convenient, please contact me immediately to reschedule.

We look forward to meeting you at NetLives.

Useful Language

We are pleased to invite you for an interview _____ .

Your interview is scheduled for _____ .

Please come to _____ .

We look forward to meeting you _____ .

Reply 3: Rejecting an Applicant

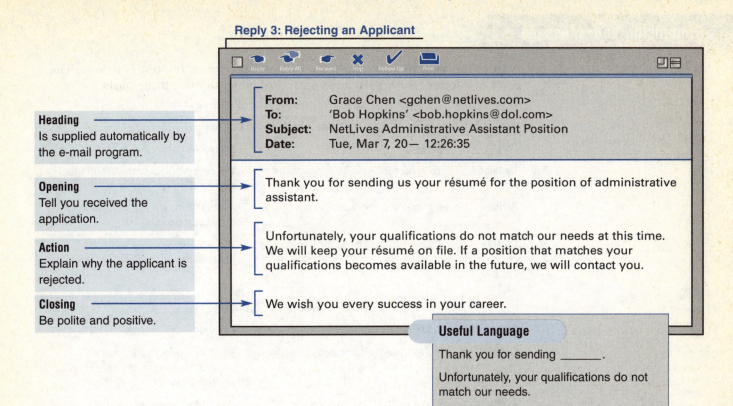

Heading
Is supplied automatically by the e-mail program.

Opening
Tell you received the application.

Action
Explain why the applicant is rejected.

Closing
Be polite and positive.

From:	Grace Chen <gchen@netlives.com>
To:	'Bob Hopkins' <bob.hopkins@dol.com>
Subject:	NetLives Administrative Assistant Position
Date:	Tue, Mar 7, 20— 12:26:35

Thank you for sending us your résumé for the position of administrative assistant.

Unfortunately, your qualifications do not match our needs at this time. We will keep your résumé on file. If a position that matches your qualifications becomes available in the future, we will contact you.

We wish you every success in your career.

Useful Language

Thank you for sending _____.

Unfortunately, your qualifications do not match our needs.

We will keep your résumé on file.

We wish you every success in your career.

Well **SAID**

When acknowledging receipt of a letter, the writer usually includes the date the letter was received. If there is a lot of correspondence, it is acceptable to acknowledge the receipt of the correspondence without the date.

That's *Good* **Business** *!*

A job applicant must always be treated with respect and kindness. People will judge your company by your response.

A letter replying to a job applicant is short and direct. Its tone is formal. The body of a letter replying to a job applicant generally has three parts.

Acknowledgment Letter

Part	Content	Example
Opening	Tell you received the application.	We received your application for the position on March 1.
Action	Explain the process.	At this time, we are reviewing the résumés. . . .
Closing	Thank the applicant for her interest.	We appreciate your interest in NetLives.

Interview Letter

Part	Content	Example
Opening	Invite the applicant for an interview.	After reviewing your résumé, we are pleased to invite you for an interview. . . .
Action	Explain what will happen.	Your interview is scheduled for Monday, March 13th at 10:00 A.M. . . .
Closing	Be enthusiastic.	We look forward to meeting you at NetLives.

Rejection Letter

Part	Content	Example
Opening	Tell you received the application.	Thank you for sending us your résumé for the position of administrative assistant.
Action	Explain why the applicant is rejected.	Unfortunately, your qualifications do not match our needs at this time. . . .
Closing	Be polite and positive.	We wish you every success in your career.

Practice 1

Write *A* if the sentence is for an acknowledgment letter, *I* for an interview letter, or *R* for a rejection letter. Some sentences may be found in more than one type of letter. Discuss your answers with your classmates.

1. **Opening**

   a. _A,I,R_ We have received your application materials for the executive assistant position.

   b. _____ After reviewing your résumé, we would like to schedule a time to meet with you.

   c. _____ We are interested in speaking further with you.

   d. _____ Thank you for applying for the position of customer service representative.

2. **Action**

    a. _____ Our human resource department is currently collecting résumés.

    b. _____ We are looking for someone with more experience.

    c. _____ We will be reviewing applications over the next few weeks.

    d. _____ If the time is not convenient, please contact me immediately.

3. **Closing**

    a. _____ I look forward to meeting you.

    b. _____ We appreciate your interest in our company.

    c. _____ We wish you much success in your job pursuit.

    d. _____ Thank you for your interest in the position.

Writing Your Message

Opening

In the opening of any business letter or e-mail, tell why you are writing. Remember to use a formal tone.

Practice 2

In each question, two of the sentences are appropriate to use in the opening of a letter replying to a job applicant. Circle the letters of the two sentences.

1. a. I received your résumé last Friday.

    b. We received your résumé yesterday.

    c. My assistant opened your application yesterday.

2. a. Thank you for applying for the executive assistant position.

    b. Thank you for trying for that executive assistant job.

    c. Thank you for your interest in the position listed in our advertisement.

3. a. Your résumé is very impressive, and I would like to schedule an interview.

    b. I would like to meet you to discuss your résumé.

    c. I want to talk with you sometime.

4. a. Thank you for responding to the advertisement.

    b. Thank you for sending your résumé.

    c. Hi! It's great that you sent your application.

5. a. I have checked out your résumé and I'm really happy to invite you for an interview.

    b. After reviewing your résumé, we would like to schedule a time to meet.

    c. Your qualifications seem to match our needs. We are pleased to arrange an interview with you.

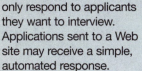

That's Good Business!

You may not receive a reply to your job application. Often, businesses get hundreds of applicants. They only respond to applicants they want to interview. Applications sent to a Web site may receive a simple, automated response.

Action

In the action part of the letter, explain the process or what will happen.

- In an acknowledgment letter, explain that someone is reviewing the materials.

- In an interview letter, suggest a specific time and date for the interview.

- In a rejection letter, explain why the applicant was not considered.

Practice 3

Match the beginning of the sentence with the appropriate ending. Then, write *A* if the sentence is for an acknowledgment letter, *I* for an interview letter, or *R* for a rejection letter. Use each ending one time.

_R_ **1.**	Your application has been carefully examined; however, _c_	**a.** is currently reviewing all files.
_____ **2.**	Our human resource department _____	**b.** invite you to talk with our General Manager.
_____ **3.**	We are pleased to _____	**c.** your experience does not match the job description.

_____ **4.**	We are in the process _____	**a.** meet with you on April 1.
_____ **5.**	We would like to _____	**b.** of collecting résumés.
_____ **6.**	Your résumé is excellent but _____	**c.** you don't have the experience necessary for the job.

_____ **7.**	We have scheduled _____	**a.** we are reviewing application materials.
_____ **8.**	At this time _____	**b.** we need someone with advanced computer skills.
_____ **9.**	Unfortunately, _____	**c.** an interview with you at 4:00 P.M. next Thursday.

_____ **10.**	We reviewed your application, but _____	**a.** schedule an interview with you.
_____ **11.**	I would like to _____	**b.** we need to hire someone with more experience.
_____ **12.**	The manager _____	**c.** is reading all cover letters and résumés.

Closing

In the closing, be positive and polite.

- In an acknowledgment letter, thank the applicant.
- In an interview letter, show your enthusiasm for the upcoming interview.
- In a rejection letter, be polite.

Practice 4   Read the sentences from job applicants. Then write appropriate closing sentences.

1. I am interested in the executive assistant position.

    Acknowledgment *Thank you for your interest in the executive assistant position.*

2. On the NetLives Web site, I read about an opening for an administrative assistant.

    Acknowledgment _____

    _____

3. I have six months of experience as an administrative assistant.

    Rejection _____

    _____

4. I meet the job requirements.

    Interview _____

    _____

5. I have been an executive secretary for more than five years.

    Interview _____

    _____

6. Although I do not have a college degree, I am a hard worker.

    Rejection _____

    _____

7. I am applying for the receptionist position announced on IronGate.com.

    Acknowledgment _____

    _____

Paul Rook is responding to the letter that you completed on page 6 in Unit 1. Complete the sentences in this letter using the information in that letter and the words below.

advertisement   openings   response   search
applicant   received   résumé   wish

Island International *Airport*

Human Resource Office
Singapore 659589

July 28, 20—

_____ (*Write your name and address here.*)

_____

_____

Dear _____: (*Write your name here.*)

Your résumé was (1) _____ and reviewed by our human

resource office. The (2) _____ to our (3) _____

was overwhelming. Unfortunately, we cannot interview every

(4) _____. We will keep your (5) _____ on file for

future (6) _____.

We (7) _____ you well in your job (8) _____.

Sincerely,

Paul Rook

Paul Rook
Human Resource Director

Maki Ishii sent an acknowledgment letter to a job applicant. The shaded boxes show ten places where she made errors. Write the correct word or punctuation above the errors.

BCL Globalcom GmbH
Goethestrasse 40113 10728 Berlin Germany

March 26, 20—

Mr. Sandy Hill
999 Pine Avenue
New Haven, CT 06540

(1), (2)   Dear Mr. Sandy Hill ,

(3)   We have received your résumé and application to the position of executive

(4), (5), (6)   asistant . We are collecting résumés later and will notified those

candidates we wish to interview.

(7)   Thank your for your interest in BCL Globalcom.

(8)   Sincerely :

Maki Ishii

(9)   Human Resource Director

(10)   Maki Ishii

The following log lists two applicants for Job Advertisement 2 on page 8 in Unit 1. The human resource department at Web Discount Corporation wants to interview only those applicants who have all three of the listed skills. Interviews should be scheduled on July 7 for one hour, between 10:00 A.M. and 2:00 P.M. On a separate piece of paper, write an acknowledgment letter to one of the applicants. Then write an interview letter or a rejection letter for the applicant.

Applicant Log			
	Skill	**Skill**	**Skill**
Job Title: Client Services Coordinator **Company Name: Web Discount Corporation**	High school or business college program	Two to four years of experience	Word processing and database experience
Akiko Yamamoto 12-A Liverpool Place London BH1 4WP United Kingdom	Y	Y	Y
John Kim 55 Havana Drive Long Beach, CA 90803	N	N	Y

Words and Expressions to Know

Look at this list of words and expressions that were used in the unit. Their definitions are in the glossary at the end of the book.

acknowledge	keep [something] on file	rejection	review
applicant	meet the requirement	reschedule	search
equivalent			

UNIT 3

Requesting a Service

When you send a letter requesting a service, you must give detailed information so the service provider can give you a complete and accurate response. Many people call the provider to discuss their needs before writing their letter. If your letter isn't detailed, you may have to write again to explain the information.

Before you write the letter, contact the people in your company who are involved with the request. Ask them if they have anything to add. Make a list or fill out a form or a log to outline your needs.

GETTING STARTED

1. Read the two e-mails about the CellFirst training seminar.
2. Complete the Planning Log.

Date: Thu, Jan 27, 20— 11:07:30
To: "Curt Marks" <cmarks@cellfirst.com>
Fr: "Pamela Davis" <pdavis@cellfirst.com>
Sub: Arrowhead East Conference Center

I got a brochure today from Arrowhead East Conference Center; I'm sending it to you by interoffice mail.

Please call them about our upcoming training seminar. The center is nearby and the rates are reasonable. See if they can accommodate 80 people. We'll need one large room and three smaller ones for break-out meetings. In the large room, we should have a microphone and a computer projection system. We'll also need lunch on the last day.

Date: Thu, Jan 27, 20— 15:07:30
To: "Pamela Davis" <pdavis@cellfirst.com>
Fr: "Curt Marks" <cmarks@cellfirst.com>
Sub: Re: Arrowhead East Conference Center

I called Jan Turner at Arrowhead East. They'll be happy to host our group on March 15 and 16. Lunch on the last day is no problem. They'll also provide coffee breaks each morning. I asked them to put five tables in each of the small rooms along with a monitor and VCR.

PLANNING LOG			
Company:	CellFirst, Inc.	**Audiovisual needs:**	
Contact person:	(1) _____	System	Number
E-mail address:	(2) _____	computer projection system	(10) _____
Phone number:	443-555-5522, ext. 23	microphone/speakers	(11) _____
Dates: arrival	(3) _____	slide projector	(12) _____
departure	(4) _____	tape recorder	(13) _____
Number of people:	(5) _____	monitor/VCR	(14) _____
Number of rooms: large	(6) _____	**Catering:**	
small	(7) _____	Meal	Date/Number of people
Furniture: tables		breakfast	(15) _____
large room	0	lunch	(16) _____
small room	(8) _____	dinner	(17) _____
chairs	(9) _____	coffee breaks	(18) _____

Look at the different elements of a letter requesting a service.

CellFirst, Inc.
10 Harbor Place Baltimore, Maryland 21220

Tel: (443) 555-5522
Fax: (443) 555-5557
www.cellfirst.com

January 28, 20—

Jan Turner
Arrowhead East Conference Center
412 Bellevue Lane
Annapolis, MD 21401

Dear Ms. Turner:

Opening

In our telephone conversation yesterday, we discussed plans to conduct our training seminar at your conference center. I would like to confirm those plans.

Focus

The dates of the seminar are March 15th and 16th. The hours are 1:00 P.M. to 6:00 P.M. on the 15th and 9:00 A.M. to 3:00 P.M. on the 16th. Eighty people will be attending. We will need a total of four rooms: one large room and three smaller break-out rooms.

As we discussed, we will need a microphone and speakers in the large room as well as a computer projection system. In each break-out room, we will need five tables, and a monitor and VCR.

Action

On March 16th, we will have a catered lunch. I would appreciate your faxing me the menu choices as soon as possible, but no later than Friday, February 4th.

I would also appreciate receiving the projected costs for our two-day meeting. You do not need to include the lunch catering costs at this time. Could you fax or e-mail me your cost projections by January 31st? I will give you final confirmation of our reservation by close-of-business on the 31st.

Closing

I want to thank you for your help in planning our seminar. I look forward to meeting you next week when I come to look over your facilities.

Best wishes,

Curt Marks

Curt Marks
Special Projects Officer
CM/ls

Useful Language

In our conversation yesterday, we discussed _____.

I would like to confirm _____.

We will need _____.

I would appreciate receiving _____.

The body of a letter requesting a service generally has four parts.

Part	Content	Example
Opening	Tell why you are writing.	In our telephone conversation yesterday, we discussed plans to conduct our training seminar at your conference center. . . .
Focus	Give details about your request.	The dates of the seminar are March 15th and 16th. The hours are 1:00 P.M. to 6:00 P.M. on the 15th and 9:00 A.M. to 3:00 P.M. on the 16th. Eighty people will be attending. We will need a total of four rooms: one large room and three smaller break-out rooms. . . .
Action	Give a time frame.	. . . Could you fax or e-mail me your cost projections by January 31st? . . .
Closing	Thank the reader and mention future communication.	I want to thank you for your help in planning our seminar. I look forward to meeting you next week. . . .

Practice 1

Write *O* if the sentence is for the opening, *F* for focus, *A* for action, or *C* for closing.

1. _____ I look forward to your response.
2. _____ We expect 25 participants.
3. _____ Please call me to confirm the rooms by next Friday.
4. _____ I'm sending you confirmation today of the details that we discussed.

5. _____ We are holding our annual meeting and I would like to get information about your facilities.
6. _____ I will get back to you by COB April 1 with the names of the participants.
7. _____ I look forward to your phone call.
8. _____ In addition to the meeting rooms, we will reserve five guest rooms.

9. _____ We now need chairs and tables for 35 attendees.
10. _____ I would like to confirm the information that we discussed on the phone today.
11. _____ We look forward to meeting with you.
12. _____ Are you available to meet on Thursday at 3:00?

13. _____ I would like you to confirm the menu by the end of the week.
14. _____ I await your confirmation.
15. _____ We will need a buffet lunch for Monday, Tuesday, and Wednesday.
16. _____ I would like to receive information about your conference facilities.

Well **SAID**

The expression *close-of-business* usually means 5:00 P.M., since most businesses are open from 9:00 A.M. to 5:00 P.M. In informal correspondence, you can use the abbreviation *COB*. (*I will fax this report by COB tomorrow.*)

Opening

In the opening of the letter, explain why you are writing. Often, when requesting a service, you are following up on a previous conversation. Make specific reference to the earlier communication.

Practice 2

Complete these sentences. Use the prepositions *at, by, for, in, of,* or *on.* Some of the prepositions may be used more than one time.

1. Thank you ___for___ your telephone call this morning.

2. We would like to hold our meeting ___at___ Barnaby Place.

3. Please e-mail the menu ___by___ Wednesday morning.

4. We will need sixty chairs ___in___ the large room.

5. I would like a list ___of___ rates for the meeting rooms.

6. The meeting will end ___on___ July 14th.

Focus

The focus of a letter requesting a service is to let the service provider know what you need. Be as clear and exact as possible.

Not clear and exact	We need *some rooms.*
Clear and exact	We will need *a total of four rooms: one large room and three smaller break-out rooms.*

Practice 3

Choose the sentence that is more clear and exact.

1. **a.** We will need a microphone and speakers.
   b. We need sound equipment.

2. **a.** Can you get back to me sometime?
   b. Could you fax or e-mail me your response tomorrow?

3. **a.** Eighty people will attend the meeting.
   b. Fewer than one hundred people will attend the meeting.

4. **a.** We are going to have a two-day meeting, March 15th and 16th.
   b. We are going to have a meeting.

5. **a.** The training seminar will take place on March 15 and 16.
   b. The training seminar will take place in March.

6. **a.** Would it be possible to have audiovisual equipment in the break-out rooms?
   b. Would it be possible to have a monitor and VCR in each of the three smaller break-out rooms?

7. **a.** We'll need a few rooms.
   b. We will need a total of four rooms.

8. **a.** Could you e-mail or fax me your cost projections by tomorrow?
   b. Could you e-mail me your cost projections ASAP?

Well **SAID**

ASAP means *as soon as possible.* Using *ASAP* means that you need something very quickly, but it doesn't give an exact date and time. If you need something done by a certain time or date, be specific.

Action

In the action part of the letter, give a time frame for some action to be done. You may promise to do something, or you may ask the recipient of the letter to do something. Again, it is important to be specific.

You also must be polite. Use *would* or *could* to ask someone to do something.

> I *would* also appreciate receiving the projected costs for our two-day meeting.

> *Could* you fax or e-mail me your costs by January 31st?

■ **Practice 4**

Rewrite these sentences as polite requests using *would* or *could*. Add your own time frame.

1. Fax me the menus. *Would you fax me the menus by May 9th?*

2. Send me the cost projections. _____

3. Provide lunch. _____

4. Open three additional rooms for break-out meetings. _____
   _____

5. Give me the price per person for coffee breaks. _____
   _____

6. Put audiovisual equipment in the three break-out rooms. _____
   _____

7. E-mail me the cost per person. _____

8. Get back to me on the dates of the training seminar. _____
   _____

9. Add two more speakers in the large room. _____
   _____

10. Tell me the total number of attendees. _____
    _____

Well SAID

Many conferences begin with a session attended by all the participants. After this session, the large group *breaks out* into smaller groups. The smaller sessions are held in *break-out* rooms.

The expression *per person* means *for each person.* For example, if the price of the coffee break is $5.00 per person and there are 100 people, the total cost of the coffee break is $500.00.

Closing

In the closing, mention some further communication. The communication may be a phone call, a meeting, a letter, a fax, or an e-mail.

■ **Practice 5**

Write sentences using the expression *I look forward to* [+ *-ing* verb]. Use each type of communication listed below. Add a specific time.

1. receiving an e-mail *I look forward to receiving your e-mail tomorrow.*

2. receiving a fax _____

3. receiving a letter _____

4. receiving a phone call _____

5. meeting _____

Complete the sentences in this letter. Use the words below.

approximately   confirm   forward   rooms
available   conversation   possible   take place

Electrical Engineering
55 Lakeshore Drive
Chicago, IL 60603

June 11, 20—

Ms. Joanne Way
California Convention and Trade Center
155 Figueroa Street
Los Angeles, CA 91335

Dear Ms. Way:

In our telephone (1) _____ this morning, we discussed the upcoming
convention of the Association of Electrical Engineering. I want to (2) _____
the following information.

The conference will (3) _____ December 3–4. We expect
(4) _____ 700 engineers and exhibitors to attend the conference.
We will need one large hall for the welcome speech and fifteen break-out
(5) _____, each with a 50-person capacity. Overhead projectors and
computers should be (6) _____ for each room.

Would it be (7) _____ for you to provide a formal lunch on the final day of
the conference? If so, please fax the menu selections to me before Friday.

I also look (8) _____ to receiving your price estimates by next Monday.
Please call me if you need additional information.

Sincerely,

John Onal

John Onal
Events Manager

Frank Feder sent a letter requesting a service. The shaded boxes show ten places where he made errors. Write the correct word or punctuation above the errors.

That's
Good Business *!*

The abbreviation *CA* stands for *California*. As a general rule, do not use abbreviations in the body of a business letter. A U.S. state name in the inside address and on the envelope are exceptions. A list of these abbreviations is on page 137.

Help the Ocean
2601 Ocean Park Avenue
Santa Monica, CA 90405

February 23, 20—

Ms. Rachel Glass
Sunburst Conference Planning
P.O. Box 61875
Monterey, CA 93940

(1) Dear Ms. Glass ;

(2) We were hold our annual meeting from May 2–5.

(3) I would like to recieve information about your meeting locations.

(4), (5) It will be twenty-five executives coming from around the world. While our

(6) will hold meetings during the day, we want to scheduled some outdoor

(7) activities. Because our organization is dedicated on the health of our
oceans, perhaps some event on the water could be arranged?

(8) Please to my attention send the materials at the above address. I will be
leaving for a business trip on March 3, so I would like to receive the
materials before I leave.

(9) I look for to hearing from you.

(10) Sincerely :

Frank Feder

Frank Feder
Director of Operations

Jan Turner, a meeting planner at Arrowhead East Conference Center, has kept a log with information from the letters requesting a service. Pretend that you are the assistant to one of the contact people below. Use the information in the log to write a letter requesting service. Remember to put your initials at the bottom of the letter after the contact person's initials.

That's Good Business!

Before reserving a meeting place, you or someone from your company should personally check out the facility. Brochures and Web sites can be misleading.

Company	WRTG Radio	Hanoi Star
Contact Person	Mary Smith	Le Ngo Quang
Address	1 Longman Plaza White Plains, NY 10606	14 Thuy Khue Tay Ho Hanoi, Vietnam
E-mail	m_smith@wrtg.com	lnq@hanoistar.net
Phone Fax	914-555-8100 914-555-8765	84-4-971-2282 84-4-971-2285
Event Dates	Sept. 15–17	Oct. 5–10
Number of Attendees	50	1000
Rooms Required		
Large		5
Small	5	25
Audiovisual Equipment		
Computer Projection System	5	5
Microphone		5
Speakers		5
Slide Projector		10
Overhead Projector		10
Monitor/VCR	5	25
Equipment		
Tables: 6' rectangular		10 per large room
Tables: 4' round		
Podium		5
Flipchart	5	25
Catering: Dates/Number of People		
Lunch	Sept. 17/50	
Dinner	Sept. 16/50	
Breaks	Sept. 16 P.M./50	

Words and Expressions to Know

Look at this list of words and expressions that were used in the unit. Their definitions are in the glossary at the end of the book.

accommodate	confirmation	look over	rate	see (find out)
confirm	fax	projected	reserve	

Confirming a Service

When you send a letter confirming a service, you must restate all of the details. The recipient needs to know that you understand the information and will fulfill the request accurately.

Before you write the letter, review all the information. If necessary, contact other people in your company who are involved. Ask them if they have anything to add. Make a list or fill out a form or a log outlining the information.

GETTING STARTED

1. Read the internal memos between the managers at Arrowhead East Conference Center about the upcoming CellFirst seminar.
2. Complete the Action Log with information about CellFirst's responses and Arrowhead's actions.

Arrowhead East Conference Center
INTEROFFICE MEMO

To: Jan Turner, Meeting Planner
From: Mark Wilson, Catering Manager
Date: February 3, 20—
Subject: Catering for CellFirst lunch

I have attached three menu choices for the March 16 lunch for the CellFirst group. I asked the client on Feb. 1 if they would prefer a buffet lunch or served lunch. They haven't gotten back to me. Could you follow up?

Arrowhead East Conference Center
INTEROFFICE MEMO

To: Mark Wilson, Catering
From: Jan Turner, Meeting Planner
cc: Janice Jackson, Audiovisual
  Tom Goode, Room Reservations
  Mary Blake, Furniture and Equipment
Date: February 4, 20—
Subject: Re: Catering for CellFirst lunch
Re: Your memo of February 3

I spoke to the client today. A buffet lunch is OK. I also asked what kind of computer they are using. They are bringing their own computer. We will provide the cables and a technician to set it up. We will provide five tables, but they have to tell us what size. We've already talked about rooms. Any other problems? Let me know.

ACTION LOG			
Department	**Contacted by Arrowhead (month/day)**	**Response from client CellFirst (month/day)**	**Action**
Room reservations	2/1	2/3	All rooms available.
Audiovisual	2/1	(1) _____	(2) _____
Furniture and equipment	2/1	?	What size tables do they need?
Catering	2/1	(3) _____	(4) _____

Look at the different elements of a letter confirming a service.

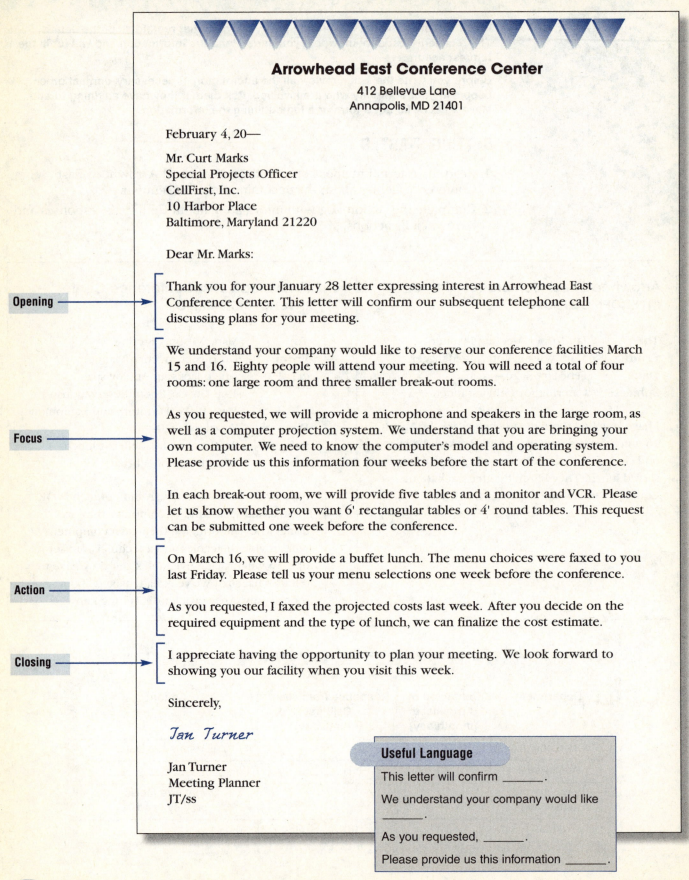

Arrowhead East Conference Center

412 Bellevue Lane
Annapolis, MD 21401

February 4, 20—

Mr. Curt Marks
Special Projects Officer
CellFirst, Inc.
10 Harbor Place
Baltimore, Maryland 21220

Dear Mr. Marks:

Opening

Thank you for your January 28 letter expressing interest in Arrowhead East Conference Center. This letter will confirm our subsequent telephone call discussing plans for your meeting.

Focus

We understand your company would like to reserve our conference facilities March 15 and 16. Eighty people will attend your meeting. You will need a total of four rooms: one large room and three smaller break-out rooms.

As you requested, we will provide a microphone and speakers in the large room, as well as a computer projection system. We understand that you are bringing your own computer. We need to know the computer's model and operating system. Please provide us this information four weeks before the start of the conference.

In each break-out room, we will provide five tables and a monitor and VCR. Please let us know whether you want 6' rectangular tables or 4' round tables. This request can be submitted one week before the conference.

Action

On March 16, we will provide a buffet lunch. The menu choices were faxed to you last Friday. Please tell us your menu selections one week before the conference.

As you requested, I faxed the projected costs last week. After you decide on the required equipment and the type of lunch, we can finalize the cost estimate.

Closing

I appreciate having the opportunity to plan your meeting. We look forward to showing you our facility when you visit this week.

Sincerely,

Jan Turner

Jan Turner
Meeting Planner
JT/ss

Useful Language

This letter will confirm _____.

We understand your company would like _____.

As you requested, _____.

Please provide us this information _____.

The body of a letter confirming a service generally has four parts.

Part	Content	Example
Opening	Tell why you are writing.	. . .This letter will confirm our subsequent telephone call discussing plans for your meeting.
Focus	Restate the client's needs completely.	We understand your company would like to reserve our conference facilities March 15 and 16. . . .
Action	Discuss problems, if any.	On March 16, we will provide a buffet lunch. The menu choices were faxed to you last Friday. Please tell us your menu selections one week before the conference. . . .
Closing	Thank the reader.	I appreciate having the opportunity to plan your meeting. . . .

Practice 1

In each question, two of the sentences are appropriate to use in a letter confirming a service. Circle the letters of the two sentences.

1. **Opening**
   a. We are pleased to confirm the plans for your conference, March 12–13.
   b. Did you need a place for your meeting?
   c. I am confirming the arrangements for your company's reception on May 11.

2. **Focus**
   a. As you outlined in your fax, we can provide six large rooms equipped with microphones and speakers.
   b. As you said on the phone, you will need one room that can be made larger or smaller.
   c. I know you need many different services for your meeting.

3. **Action**
   a. Please let us know a week before your conference begins whether you will need a technician's assistance.
   b. Our meeting rooms are very large.
   c. We will fax the price estimates to you today.

4. **Closing**
   a. We thank you for this opportunity to serve you.
   b. I will fax the estimates tomorrow.
   c. We are happy that you have chosen Sunburst as your event planner.

That's
Good Business!

Look at the second memo on page 27. The letters *cc* mean *carbon copy*. When you put a name after *cc*, it means that the person gets a copy of the e-mail or letter because it contains important information.

Personal Pronouns

Personal pronouns refer to something or someone mentioned before. In the model letter on page 28, Jan Turner is writing to Curt Marks.

> Thank *you* for *your* January 28 letter expressing interest in Arrowhead East Conference Center.
>
> you = Curt Marks   your = Curt Marks's (letter)
>
> This letter will confirm *our* subsequent telephone call discussing plans for *your* meeting.
>
> our = Jan Turner and the Arrowhead staff's (plans)
> your = Curt Marks and the CellFirst staff's (meeting)

Practice 2   Underline the personal pronouns in these sentences from the model letter. Write whether the pronouns refer to Marks, Turner, Turner/Arrowhead, or Marks/CellFirst.

1. We understand <u>your</u> company would like to reserve <u>our</u> conference facilities.
   Marks   *Turner/Arrowhead*

2. As you requested, we will provide a microphone and speakers.

3. Please provide us this information.

4. As you requested, I faxed the projected costs last week.

5. I appreciate the opportunity to plan your meeting.

Sentence Order

The order of sentences in a paragraph helps the reader understand the meaning. Usually, a general statement or a restatement of the request comes before a specific statement about the request.

> We will provide five tables and a monitor and VCR. Please let us know whether you want 6' rectangular tables or 4' round tables.

Practice 3   Match the general restatement with the specific statement.

   a. We will provide a VCR in each room.
   b. There will be a computer projection system in the auditorium.
   c. Coffee breaks will be provided between the morning sessions.
   d. You requested five rooms for your meetings.
   e. You will need 50 chairs.

1. __*b*__ We need your computer's model and operating system by Friday.

2. _____ We will need to know the day before the conference whether you would like the chairs set up theater style or horseshoe style.

3. _____ Let us know Monday which VCR format (NSTC or PAL) you need.

4. _____ We have rooms in four different sizes: rooms for 10, 30, 60, or 100 people. Which sizes would meet your needs?

5. _____ We can also provide cake and cookies at this time. Please complete the catering request form and send it to us by June 3.

Whether . . . or, either . . . or, and *if*

When you give a choice to a client, you must be clear. *Whether . . . or, either . . . or,* and *if* are used in sentences with a choice.

> Please let us know *whether* you want 6' rectangular tables *or* 4' round tables.

Practice 4   Write sentences that give choices for these general restatements.

1. We will provide lunch on the first day. (buffet or served lunch)

   Please let us know whether you want a buffet or a served lunch. or

   You can have either a buffet or a served lunch. or

   Please let us know if you want a buffet or a served lunch.

2. There will be two tables in each room. (rectangular or round)

   _____

3. You requested a VCR for each break-out room. (NSTC or PAL format)

   _____

4. I am faxing you menus for the three meals and coffee breaks. (coffee breaks in morning, afternoon, or both)

   _____

5. We will put 100 chairs in the large room. (theater style or horseshoe style)

   _____

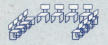
Gerunds and Infinitives

Some verbs can be followed by the *–ing* (gerund) form of a verb. Some verbs can be followed by the *to* (infinitive) form of a verb. Some verbs can be followed by either. In addition, a phrase that ends in a preposition (such as *to, in, of, on, for,* or *at*) is always followed by the gerund form.

> I appreciate *having* the opportunity *to plan* your meeting.
>   gerund   infinitive

> We look forward to *showing* you our facility when you visit this week.
>   gerund

Practice 5   Complete the sentences below with the correct form of the verb.

1. I want to thank you for ___*letting*___ Arrowhead plan your meeting.
               (let)

   We look forward to _____ you our facility.
                    (show)

2. Arrowhead tries hard _____ and keep your loyalty. If you have
                    (win)

   any questions, please do not hesitate _____ me.
                        (contact)

3. If you need _____ any changes, please call me immediately.
            (make)

4. I enjoy _____ people to our facility and I look forward to
         (introduce)

   _____ you a personal tour.
      (give)

5. Our staff is _____ sure everything happens on schedule.
            (make)

Complete the sentences in this letter. Use the words below.

as well as	contact	discussions	place
attached	deciding	In addition	selected

Arrowhead East Conference Center

412 Bellevue Lane
Annapolis, MD 21401

April 17, 20—

Mr. Mark Foster
E-Z Network Communications
23232 Greens Lane
Reston, VA 22096

Dear Mr. Foster:

We are pleased that you have (1) _____ Arrowhead East Conference Center to host your training seminar. This letter will confirm our understanding of our telephone (2) _____.

The seminar will take (3) _____ on June 3. You are expecting 35 participants and will need one large room with six 4' round tables and 35 chairs. (4) _____, you will require a computer projection system, (5) _____ a flip chart.

This morning, our catering manager, Virginia Wu, faxed the menu choices for your lunch on the 3rd. She will call you tomorrow to discuss these options with you.

I have (6) _____ a projected cost for your seminar. If you have any questions, please do not hesitate to (7) _____ me.

We understand that you have choices when (8) _____ where to hold your seminar. I'm sure you will be pleased that you chose Arrowhead.

Sincerely,

Jan Turner

Jan Turner
Meeting Planner
JT/ss

Alicia Rosas sent a letter confirming a service. The shaded boxes show ten places where she made errors. Write the correct word or punctuation above the errors.

That's Good Business!

Look at the initials *AR/ab* at the bottom of this letter. The capital letters are the initials of Alicia Rosas, who wrote and signed the letter. The lowercase letters are the initials of the person who typed the letter.

Sunburst Conference Planning

P.O. Box 61875
Monterey, CA 93940

August 10, 20—

Mr. Jim Kraft
Moran Products
10023 Commonwealth Avenue
Monterey, CA 93942

(1) Dear Mr Kraft:

(2) We are pleased to confirming the arrangements for your November 24–26
(3) conferance at Sunburst.

(4) As you indication on the phone, you are expecting between 200 and 300 people
(5) for the three-day event. We will reserved a room that can be closed off or opened
(6) up to accommodate the final number of people. You say you will provide your
(7) own audiovisual equipment, but if you need anything on the last minute, we have
equipment available.

We understand you will not need any catering. Should you change your mind,
(8) please let us know before November 20?

(9) I have attached a projection cost for your review. Please call me if anything needs
further explanation.

(10) Again, I want to thank you for to choose Sunburst. I'm sure you will be pleased
with the quality of service we offer.

Sincerely,

Alicia Rosas

Alicia Rosas
Events Manager
AR/ab

On a separate piece of paper, write a response to one of the following requests for service.

That's Good Business!

In most correspondence, feet are abbreviated with the symbol '. Inches are abbreviated with the symbol ". For example, 6' 2" means six feet and two inches.

Client A	Client B
Ms. K. Miura Hatorri Trading Co. Ltd. 4-1, Okana 1-chome Midori-ku Yokohama 226-8525 Japan	Mr. Julian Wateau Madrange Carbon 15 bis, rue A. Dehodencq 75416 Paris France

Requests		
	Client A	Client B
Purpose	seminar	conference
Dates	March 10	March 11–12
Number of participants	20	300
Room reservations	1 large 3 small	2 large
Audiovisual	computer projection	speakers and microphone
Equipment	four 4' round tables	chairs in theater style
Catering	lunch	none

Words and Expressions to Know

Look at this list of words and expressions that were used in the unit. Their definitions are in the glossary at the end of the book.

estimate   expect   indicate   negotiable   restate

UNIT 5

Ordering Supplies

All businesses order supplies. Supplies include many different items: computers, parts for assembly, and pens and pencils, for example. It is very important for businesses to have supplies when they need them. When you need supplies, first call the vendor to discuss price and availability. Then send a letter with a formal purchase order.

Before you write the letter and complete the purchase order, make sure you know exactly what items you need and on what dates you need them.

GETTING STARTED

1. Read the note about components that need to be ordered from Component Outsource Ltd. Then look at the production schedule. It is important that both the quantities and the dates are accurate.
2. Complete Purchase Order 113512.

From the Desk of M. Simpson

10/24

Mark,

I received this production schedule from the factory that assembles our computers. Yesterday, I talked to Ms. Chen, our supplier from Component Outsource, Ltd. I told her that our stock date has to be 10 days before our assembly start dates. She said she'll waive shipping costs and give us a 10% discount.

Please make up a purchase order for the chip sets and drives, and order today.

MS

Production Schedule: Computer Assembly			
Computer Model	Assembly Start Date	Component Chip Sets*	Component Drives*
G34	02/15	Intex 440SX	Ultra ATA/88
SUX600	02/15	AGB 5/x/233	Ultra ATA/88
550 PL	03/15	Intex 600	Ardo 6L
PC1000x	03/15	Intex 440SX	Ardo 6L

*50,000 of each component required per model.

PURCHASE ORDER 113512

Component	Quantity	Unit price/ thousand	Cost	Cost less 10% discount	Stock date (month/day)
Intex 440SX	100,000	$500	$50,000	$45,000	02/05
AGB 5/x/233	50,000	$800	$40,000	(6) _____	(9) _____
Intex 600	(1) _____	$500	(3) _____	$22,500	(10) _____
Ultra ATA/88	100,000	$1,000	$100,000	(7) _____	02/05
Ardo 6L	(2) _____	$1,000	(4) _____	(8) _____	03/05
TOTAL	n/a	n/a	(5) _____	$283,500	n/a

Deliver by stock date to:

Mr. Walter Granger
Shipping and Receiving Department
Dalway Computers
Address on file

Send invoice to:

Ms. Marcia Collins
Accounting Department
Dalway Computers
Address on file

Look at the different elements of a fax ordering supplies.

FAX

Dalway Computers

Jl. Barito II, No. 48
Kby baru
Jakarata 11001, Indonesia
Phone: (021) 5200357
Fax: (021) 5493794
info@dalway.com.id

To:	Ms. Jackie Chen
Title:	Export Manager
Company:	Component Outsource Ltd.
Address:	50 Orchard Road
	Singapore 238865
Telephone:	(65) 735 58 09
Fax:	(65) 735 58 11
Pages:	Cover plus 1
Date:	November 24, 20—
Ref:	Customer Number: DC 43223-A

Dear Ms. Chen:

Opening

I am sending by fax Purchase Order 113512 for the following chip sets and drives.

Chip sets	100,000	Intex 440 SX
	50,000	AGB 5/x/233
	50,000	Intex 600
Drives	100,000	Ultra ATA/88
	100,000	Ardo 6L

Focus

These components should arrive no later than the stock dates noted in the purchase order. Delivery instructions are detailed in the purchase order.

Action

As you discussed in your November 23 telephone conversation with M. Simpson, you offered to waive shipping costs and to give a 10 percent discount. We appreciate the offer and, as with previous orders, will pay upon receipt of an invoice and the components. Invoicing instructions are detailed in the purchase order.

Closing

If you have any questions concerning our order, please do not hesitate to contact me.

Sincerely,

Mark Wu

Mark Wu
Purchasing Specialist

Useful Language

I am sending _____.

Instructions are detailed in _____.

We will pay upon receipt _____.

If you have any questions concerning _____.

The body of a fax ordering supplies generally has four parts.

Part	Content	Example
Opening	Tell what you are ordering.	I am sending by fax Purchase Order 113512 for the following chip sets and drives.
Focus	Tell when you need the item. Tell how to deliver the item.	These components should arrive no later than the stock dates noted in the purchase order. Delivery instructions are detailed in the purchase order.
Action	Tell how you will pay for the item	As you discussed in your November 23 telephone conversation with M.Simpson, you offered to waive shipping costs and to give a 10 percent discount. We appreciate the offer and, as with previous orders, will pay upon receipt of an invoice and the components. . . .
Closing	Ask them to contact you if necessary.	If you have any questions concerning our order, please do not hesitate to contact me.

Practice 1

In each question, two of the sentences are appropriate to use in a letter ordering supplies. Circle the letters of the two sentences.

1. Opening

   a. I have enclosed Purchase Order A-342 for 50,000 hard drives.

   b. To confirm our telephone conversation, I am sending Purchase Order 85-3425 for the following items.

   c. Could you send me some chip sets, please?

2. Focus

   a. The items should be shipped to arrive no later than March 15.

   b. Are these items in stock?

   c. We would appreciate receiving the items as soon as possible, but no later than April 15.

3. Action

   a. Let us know how much we owe.

   b. As we agreed, your invoice will be paid 30 days after delivery of the chips and drives.

   c. Your invoice will be processed upon receipt of the components.

4. Closing

   a. We appreciate your cooperation in filling our order.

   b. You're not the only supplier, so do a good job for us.

   c. We look forward to continued good relations with Component Outsource Ltd.

The Body of an Order Fax

When you place an order, you must be very precise. Give the reader all the information needed to fill the order.

What	What items do you want to order?
How	How many items are you ordering?
When	When do you need the items?
Who	Who will receive the order?
Who	Who will receive the invoice?
When	When will the invoice be paid?

Practice 2 Answer the questions. Use the purchase order on page 35 and the model fax on page 36.

1. What items did Mr. Wu order? _____

2. How many of each did he order? _____

3. When does he need the items? _____

4. Who will receive the shipment of components? _____

5. Who will receive the invoice for the components? _____

6. When will the invoice be paid? _____

Opening

The opening tells the reader exactly why you are writing. Be very specific.

Practice 3 Complete these opening sentences for a fax ordering supplies. Use the prepositions *of*, *for*, *on*, and *with*. Use each preposition one time.

1. I am sending purchase order 64-321 along _____ the completed credit reference form.

2. Our order _____ 50,000 drives, model number AB-3, is enclosed.

3. We are canceling our order _____ June 3.

4. As we discussed _____ the phone this morning, I am sending purchase order 4858D for 10,000 chip sets.

Focus

You must also be very specific with delivery details. Compare these sentences.

General	We need the components *next week*.
Specific	These components *should arrive no later than the stock dates noted in the purchase order*.

Here are some prepositions and prepositional phrases that are used for deadlines:

before   by   no later than   on or before

Rewrite these general statements. Replace the underlined word or phrase with specific times and dates. Use the prepositions and prepositional phrases on page 38 and add your own specific times and dates.

1. Please deliver the product <u>ASAP</u>.

   Please deliver the product by COB January 10th.

2. We look forward to receiving the chip sets <u>soon</u>.

   _____

3. The components should be sent to our warehouse <u>in a few days</u>.

   _____

4. It is important that the goods be received <u>in the near future</u>.

   _____

5. The items must be on hand <u>next month</u>.

   _____

Action

The customer and the vendor usually agree on the payment method before the customer places the order. The order letter confirms the payment method. Some expressions beginning with *as* are used to discuss facts that both people already know. When you begin a sentence with one of these expressions, use a comma.

> *As you discussed* in your November 23 telephone conversation with M. Simpson, you offered to waive shipping costs and to give a 10 percent discount.

Here are some expressions using *as*:

As usual,	As we discussed,
As we agreed,	As we have done in the past,

■ **Practice 5**

Rewrite these sentences using one of the *as* expressions.

1. We talked about paying within 30 days of receipt of the invoice.

   As we discussed, we will pay within 30 days of receipt of the invoice.

2. We always pay upon receipt of the goods in satisfactory condition.

   _____

3. During our meeting we agreed to send a deposit of half the amount and pay the balance when the goods are delivered.

   _____

4. Last time we paid by credit card when we placed the order.

   _____

5. You requested we enclose a completed credit reference form.

   _____

That's
Good **Business !**

A telephone call or e-mail is a good way to discuss options and to make decisions on costs, payment methods, and other negotiable items. A letter confirms arrangements made on the telephone. This confirmation gives everybody all the information in writing.

Complete the sentences in this letter. Use the words below.

balance	Delivery	following	order
concerning	enclosed	items	submit

Guangzhou Exports
No. 6 Shamian South Street
Guangzhou 510133
Phone (86-20) 8120-8777
Fax (86-20) 8120-8778

March 18, 20—

Ms. Carmen Santana
Go Manufacturing
Western Industrial Zone
Guangzhou 511356

Dear Ms. Santana:

I am enclosing Purchase Order A-53 for the (1) _____

office supplies:

            10 boxes of printer paper

            5 boxes of #10 envelopes

We would like these (2) _____ delivered no later than

Monday afternoon. (3) _____ instructions are on the

(4) _____ purchase order.

As usual, please apply the total of this (5) _____ against our

credit line. We will pay the (6) _____ at the end of the month

when you (7) _____ an invoice.

If you have any questions (8) _____ our order, please do not

hesitate to contact me.

Sincerely yours,

John Yu

John Yu
Purchasing Supervisor

Enclosure

Letter Practice 2

Marcia Wess sent an e-mail ordering supplies. The shaded boxes show ten places where she made errors. Write the correct word or punctuation above the errors.

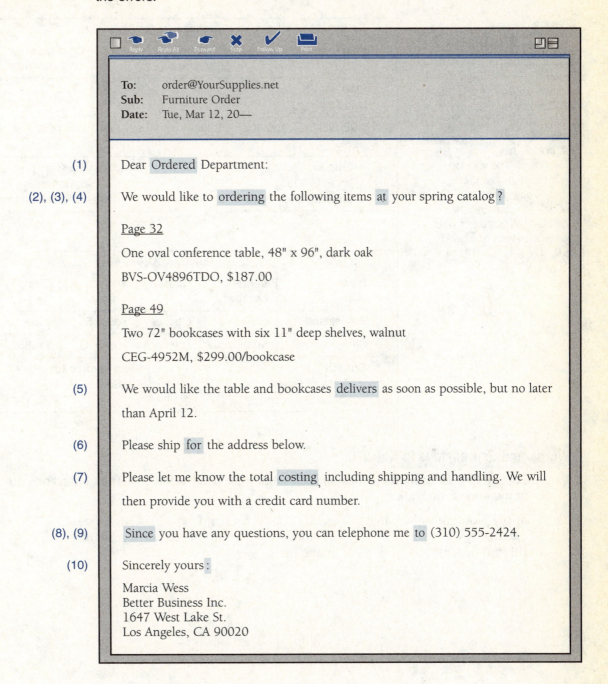

(1)

Dear Ordered Department:

(2), (3), (4)

We would like to ordering the following items at your spring catalog?

Page 32
One oval conference table, 48" x 96", dark oak
BVS-OV4896TDO, $187.00

Page 49
Two 72" bookcases with six 11" deep shelves, walnut
CEG-4952M, $299.00/bookcase

(5)

We would like the table and bookcases delivers as soon as possible, but no later than April 12.

(6)

Please ship for the address below.

(7)

Please let me know the total costing, including shipping and handling. We will then provide you with a credit card number.

(8), (9)

Since you have any questions, you can telephone me to (310) 555-2424.

(10)

Sincerely yours :

Marcia Wess
Better Business Inc.
1647 West Lake St.
Los Angeles, CA 90020

To: order@YourSupplies.net
Sub: Furniture Order
Date: Tue, Mar 12, 20—

On a separate piece of paper, order the supplies listed in one of the following purchase orders. Look in your local telephone book or on the Internet for addresses to use in your letter.

That's Good Business!

Vendors sometimes ask new customers to complete a credit reference form before they will fill orders. The vendor sends the form to a credit agency. The agency tells the vendor if the customer has good credit. A customer who pays bills on time has good credit.

Purchase Order AX-36-443

Item	Quantity	Unit price/ thousand	Cost	Cost less 10% discount	Stock date (month/day)
Intex 440SX chip sets	50,000	$100	$5,000	$4,500	06/18
AGB 5/x/233 drives	100,000	$200	$20,000	$18,000	06/18

Ship to:	Send invoice to:
Mr. Peter Liu Shipping and Receiving Department	Mr. Max Gonzales Accounting Department

Purchase Order 8940

Item	Item number	Quantity	Unit price	Cost	Stock date (month/day)
File folders	ESS-128	6 boxes	$25.50	$153	03/24
Stick-on notes	MMM-7662	100 packs	$13.85	$1385	03/24

Ship to:	Send invoice to:
Melanie Brown Office Services	Same

Words and Expressions to Know

Look at this list of words and expressions that were used in the unit. Their definitions are in the glossary at the end of the book.

apply [something] against   goods   on hand   process
balance   in stock   pay upon receipt   waive
fill [an] order   make up

Confirming an Order

When you send a letter confirming an order, be specific. Give any additional information about the order, such as items that are out of stock or on back order.

Before you write the letter, make sure that you can fulfill the order. If there is a problem with availability or schedule, write about it in the letter.

GETTING STARTED

1. Read the following fax and the e-mail response to the fax. The export manager at Component Outsource Ltd. found out about a delay in the shipment they expect from A-Tech Inc. Some of the orders Computer Outsource has to ship will be delayed.
2. Complete the Order Log. Write a check (✔) next to the names of the customers who have to be contacted about the shipping problem.

A-Tech Inc.
Chip Manufacturing Division

19-3 Banpo-dong
Seocho-Ku
Seoul 137-040
Korea

82-2-6284-6566   Telephone
82-2-6284-7700   Fax
info@atech.com   E-mail

FAX TRANSMISSION

Fax: (65) 735 58 11
Pages: 1

Date: December 3, 20—

To: Ms. Jackie Chen
         Export Manager
         Component Outsource Ltd.
         Telephone: (65) 735 58 09

From: Yon Mi Lee
         Production Supervisor

Ref: Your November 28 order
Subj: Shipping Delay

We regret to inform you that the Intex 440SX chip sets will not be shipped as scheduled. They will be shipped on February 1st. All other chip sets will be delivered on time. We apologize for any inconvenience this delay may cause.

To:	J. Wilson <jwilson@ComponentOut.com>
Fr:	J. Chen <jchen@ComponentOut.com>
Sub:	Delay of Intex 440SX
Date:	Fri, Dec 3, 20—

I received a fax from A-Tech this morning. They're going to be a week behind schedule for the Intex 440SX shipment. Please call the customers who ordered this chip set, then fax a confirmation letter about the delay. Ask if we can substitute AGB 5/x/233. We have those chip sets on hand.

ORDER LOG				
Customer	__ Dalway Computers	__ Dalway Computers	__ Midway Graphics	__ Tiger Industrials
Customer number	DC 43223-A	DC 43223-A	DE 23321-A	DD 01244-C
Component	Intex 440SX	Intex 600	Intex 600	Intex 440SX
Quantity	100,000	50,000	450,000	200,000
Order date (month/day)	11/24	11/24	11/10	11/10
Ship date (month/day)	01/15	02/15	03/15	03/15

Look at the different elements of a letter confirming an order.

Component Outsource Ltd.

350 Orchard Road
Singapore 238865
Telephone (65) 735 58 09
Fax (65) 735 58 11

December 3, 20—

Mr. Mark Wu
Dalway Computers
Jl. Barito II, No. 48
Kby baru
Jakarta 11001, Indonesia

Ref: Purchase Order 113512 of November 24

Dear Mr. Wu:

Opening → We received your November 24 fax and Purchase Order 113512. We are pleased to supply the components you requested on the dates specified, with the exception noted below.

Focus → As we discussed in our phone call this morning, the chip set Intex 440SX is not in stock.

Action → We will back order this item and will ship it on February 5.

Closing → If I can be of further assistance, please do not hesitate to call. Your business is very important to us, and we look forward to serving you in the future.

Sincerely yours,

John Wilson

John Wilson
Product Manager

Useful Language

We received your _____ fax and Purchase Order _____.

We are pleased to supply _____.

As we discussed, _____ is not in stock.

If I can be of further assistance, _____.

Your business is very important to us.

The body of a letter confirming an order generally has four parts.

Part	Content	Example
Opening	Refer to the specific order and the date it was sent or arrived.	We received your November 24 fax and Purchase Order 113512. . . .
Focus	State the problem, if any.	As we discussed in our phone call this morning, the chip set Intex 440SX is not in stock.
Action	Tell what you plan to do.	We will back order this item and will ship it on February 5.
Closing	Thank the reader.	If I can be of further assistance, please do not hesitate to call. Your business is very important to us, and we look forward to serving you in the future.

Practice 1

Circle the letter of the sentence that is most similar to the sentence in the Model Letter: Confirming an Order on page 44.

1. **Opening**
   a. Your e-mail ordering office furniture was received.
   b. We are pleased to confirm your order for the office supplies listed in your letter of May 3.
   c. We got your order.

2. **Focus**
   a. We don't have any left.
   b. Item number OSD-32 is very popular this year.
   c. In our telephone conversation, I offered you a choice between 10- or 20-pound copy paper.

3. **Action**
   a. You'll get the items eventually.
   b. We will substitute the oak for the walnut desk.
   c. We will ship the items in stock and will ship the back-ordered items no later than May 15.

4. **Closing**
   a. Our products are the best in the business.
   b. We are having a special sale at the end of the month. Please call customer service if you would like a catalog.
   c. If there's any way we can improve our service, please do not hesitate to tell us.

That's Good Business!

It is important to be very polite and apologetic to customers when there is a problem with their order. You want your customers to be happy. Unhappy customers might go to another vendor.

The Subject or Reference Line

In many business letters and in all e-mails, there is a line that tells the reader what the focus of the letter is. This is called the subject line or the reference line. It is important that this line be clear and concise.

> Ref: Purchase Order 113512 of November 24

Practice 2 Write a check (✔) next to the phrases that are good subject or reference lines.

1. _____ Your order

2. _____ G. Barton's fax of June 12

3. _____ Back-ordered items

4. _____ Our August 15 telephone conversation

5. _____ PO 466-43A

6. _____ What are we going to do about PO 684?

7. _____ Out-of-stock item: ODD-344 oak desk

8. _____ Fax

Opening

The opening of the confirmation letter repeats the information found in the subject or reference line. Here are some phrases that are used in an opening paragraph.

> *We received* your November 24 fax and Purchase Order 113512.
> *Your letter of June 6 arrived* today.
> *In response to* your e-mail of May 10, we are confirming your order.
> *This letter confirms* the receipt of your faxed Purchase Order 34-442.
> *Thank you for* your letter of January 13.

Practice 3 Write an opening sentence for a letter or an e-mail with these subject or reference lines. Use each of the phrases above one time.

1. Ref: Your Purchase Order X-32BA of June 10

   We received your Purchase Order X-32 BA of June 10.

2. Re: Your furniture order of September 6

   _____

3. Sub: Your e-mail of August 10

   _____

4. Sub: Your fax and purchase order of March 2

   _____

5. Re: Your order letter of January 9

   _____

That's Good Business!

The words *subject* and *reference* are often abbreviated when they appear at the top of letters, faxes, and e-mails.

Subject   Subj: or Sub:
Reference Ref: or Re:

If the customer is angry about a problem, you should call rather than just send a letter. Follow up the telephone call with a letter. In the letter, refer to the phone conversation. Here are some common phrases often used at the beginning of a sentence to refer to a previous meeting or conversation.

As we discussed in our phone call this morning, the chip set Intex 440SX is not in stock.

As I told you in our telephone conversation today, we are unable to fill your order at this time.

In our meeting yesterday, I told you that the desk is not available in oak.

Practice 4   Combine the two sentences into one sentence. Use the phrases above.

1. We had a meeting Friday. I told you that the #5 pens are back ordered.
   In our meeting Friday, I told you that the #5 pens are back ordered.

2. We talked on the phone this morning. Intex chip sets are out of stock.

   _____

   _____

3. Our telephone conversation was last week. All items on your purchase order are no longer in production.

   _____

   _____

4. We spoke in my office Monday. We are unable to fill your order at this time.

   _____

   _____

(Action

When there is a problem, you must give a solution.

Problem   Chip set Intex 440SX is not in stock.

Solution   *We will back order this item and will ship it on February 5.*

Practice 5   Write the letter of the solution that best solves the problem.

Problems

1. All components are out of stock. _____
2. The bookcase is not available in white. _____
3. Item ODS, printer paper, is back ordered. _____
4. The items you ordered are available only in larger quantities. _____

Solutions

a. We have it in brown and black.
b. We will ship the larger quantities, but charge you only for the number you ordered.
c. It will be in stock by June 10.
d. We will forward them to you as soon as they are available.

Complete the sentences in this letter. Use the words below.

additional   fax   in stock   ordered
anything   important   number   requested

West Virginia Office Supplies
220 First Ave.
Morgantown, WV 26506

March 3, 20—

Javier Perez
Office Manager
Winston and Peras, LP
1400 16th Street, Suite 330
Washington, DC 20036-1301

Re: Purchase Order 6453

Dear Mr. Perez:

Thank you for your (1) _____ and Purchase Order 6453. All of
the items are (2) _____ and will be shipped overnight as you
(3) _____.

You (4) _____ 100 black pens, stock number 3245. As we
discussed on the telephone, these pens now come in boxes of twelve. We
will send you 10 boxes of twelve for no (5) _____ charge.

Your business is very (6) _____ to us. If we can do
(7) _____ else for you, please call me at my toll-free
(8) _____, (888) 555-2323, ext. 24, or e-mail me at
rnair@wvoffice.com.

Sincerely yours,

Rajan Nair

Rajan Nair
Account Manager

That's
Good Business!

Be sure to tell
people how to
contact you.
Most business
stationery
includes a
phone number, fax number,
e-mail address, and mailing
address. If your stationery
does not include this
information, add it to the
body of your letter or
beneath where you type
your name and title.

Nguyen Tan sent an e-mail confirming an order. The shaded boxes show ten places where he made errors. Write the correct word or punctuation above the errors.

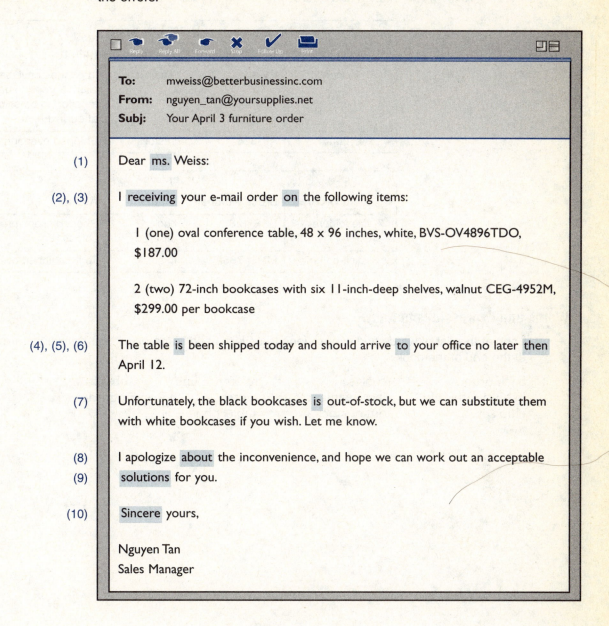

To: mweiss@betterbusinessinc.com
From: nguyen_tan@yoursupplies.net
Subj: Your April 3 furniture order

(1) Dear ms. Weiss:

(2), (3) I receiving your e-mail order on the following items:

    1 (one) oval conference table, 48 x 96 inches, white, BVS-OV4896TDO, $187.00

    2 (two) 72-inch bookcases with six 11-inch-deep shelves, walnut CEG-4952M, $299.00 per bookcase

(4), (5), (6) The table is been shipped today and should arrive to your office no later then April 12.

(7) Unfortunately, the black bookcases is out-of-stock, but we can substitute them with white bookcases if you wish. Let me know.

(8) I apologize about the inconvenience, and hope we can work out an acceptable
(9) solutions for you.

(10) Sincere yours,

Nguyen Tan
Sales Manager

On a separate piece of paper, write a letter to confirm the orders listed in one of the following order logs. Look in your local telephone book or on the Internet for names and addresses to use in your letter.

Order Log 827-A			
Item Ordered	Stock Number	Status	Action
17" monitor	PV-17	unavailable	In phone conversation yesterday, client agreed to upgrade to 21" monitor; to be shipped overnight at our expense.
keyboard	AP-324	in stock	Shipped overnight.

Order Log 76889			
Item Ordered	Stock Number	Status	Action
file folders	ESS-128	back ordered	Phoned client; promised to ship 2/12.
stick-on notes	MMM-7662	in stock	To be shipped overnight.

Words and Expressions to Know

Look at this list of words and expressions that were used in the unit. Their definitions are in the glossary at the end of the book.

back order	concise	reference line	substitute
behind schedule	inconvenience	regret	upgrade
chip set	out of stock	subject line	

UNIT 7

Requesting Information

When you send a letter requesting information, you usually want to find out something that was not included in a newspaper article, a company Web site, or other source.

Before you write the letter, organize your information so you know what to ask. In your letter, you may mention where you heard about something, so be sure to keep a record of where and when you got your information.

GETTING STARTED

1. Read the newspaper article, the e-mail, and the Web site about the XL-Lite digital camera.
2. Complete the New Product Information Chart. Include the source of the information. Write *N* if the source is the newspaper article, *E* if it is the e-mail, *W* if it is the Web site, or *?* if the information is not given. If there is more than one source, list all sources.

NEW YORK—Click Camera Company Announces New Camera.
Today Click Camera Company announced a new addition to their digital camera line. The camera, called XL-Lite, takes pictures without light. This feature will appeal to the home photographer taking pictures in low-light situations. The camera also has a long-life battery and can take up to 260 digital images.

Subject:	Boston Daily News article
To:	b_gomez@camara.com.pe
From:	s_sanchez@camara.com.pe
Date:	Fri, Mar 17, 20— 10:42:51 AM

Did you read the article about the XL-Lite, the new digital camera? It's going to be on the market in the fall. I heard it would take 80 images at high resolution and up to 260 at low resolution. I don't have time to check the Web site for more information. Could you check it out?

Address: @ http://www.click.net

New Product **Click Camera Company XL-Lite Digital Camera** BUY NOW

- Compact body, 270 g (9.5 oz.)
- 2x Optical zoom lens
- Digital interface: USB and serial
- Low light sensitivity
- Three power sources
  → lithium battery
  → rechargeable battery
  → AC adapter

Questions? E-mail us for more information.

NEW PRODUCT INFORMATION CHART

Company	*Click Camera Company*	*N, W*
Product	(1) _____	_____
Brand	(2) _____	_____
Availability	(3) _____	_____
Compact body	(4) _____	_____
Zoom lens	(5) _____	_____
Power sources	(6) _____	_____
Number of digital images		
• Low resolution	(7) _____	_____
• High resolution	(8) _____	_____
Price	(9) _____	_____
Sales discount	(10) _____	_____
Promotional materials	(11) _____	_____
More information	(12) _____	_____

Look at the different elements of an e-mail requesting information.

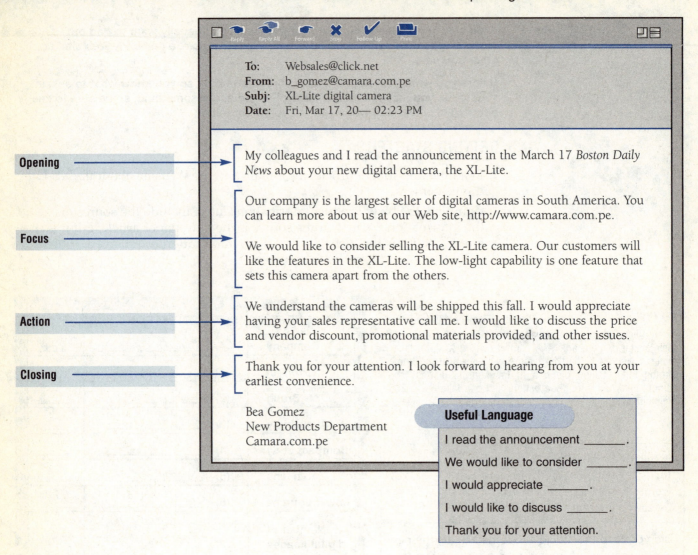

Opening

To: Websales@click.net
From: b_gomez@camara.com.pe
Subj: XL-Lite digital camera
Date: Fri, Mar 17, 20— 02:23 PM

My colleagues and I read the announcement in the March 17 *Boston Daily News* about your new digital camera, the XL-Lite.

Focus

Our company is the largest seller of digital cameras in South America. You can learn more about us at our Web site, http://www.camara.com.pe.

We would like to consider selling the XL-Lite camera. Our customers will like the features in the XL-Lite. The low-light capability is one feature that sets this camera apart from the others.

Action

We understand the cameras will be shipped this fall. I would appreciate having your sales representative call me. I would like to discuss the price and vendor discount, promotional materials provided, and other issues.

Closing

Thank you for your attention. I look forward to hearing from you at your earliest convenience.

Bea Gomez
New Products Department
Camara.com.pe

Useful Language

I read the announcement _____.

We would like to consider _____.

I would appreciate _____.

I would like to discuss _____.

Thank you for your attention.

That's Good Business!

Look at the e-mail on page 51. An interoffice e-mail or an e-mail between close associates does not have to look like a letter. You can type your message in the space without a greeting or a signature.

If you are sending an e-mail to someone you don't know, you should be more formal. You can use a letter format in your e-mail, including a greeting and signature, or you can use a memo format.

Many e-mail programs add an automatic signature. Your name, contact information, and sometimes a scanned signature can be automatically placed at the bottom of each e-mail.

The body of an e-mail requesting information generally has four parts.

Part	Content	Example
Opening	Tell why you are writing.	My colleagues and I read the announcement in the March 17 *Boston Daily News* about your new digital camera, the XL-Lite.
Focus	Tell who you are.	Our company is the largest seller of digital cameras in South America. . . .
Action	Tell what you need to know.	We understand the cameras will be shipped this fall. I would appreciate having your sales representative call me. I would like to discuss the price and vendor discount, promotional materials provided, and other issues.
Closing	Thank them for their assistance.	Thank you for your attention. I look forward to hearing from you at your earliest convenience.

Practice 1

In each question, two of the sentences are appropriate to use in a letter requesting information. Circle the letters of the two sentences.

1. **Opening**
   a. We have learned from our supplier, Marcus Auto Parts, Inc., that you are producing a new car radio.
   b. What's new?
   c. In the September issue of *Business Travel Express*, you announced the opening of your new hotel.

2. **Focus**
   a. For forty-five years, we have supplied schools around the world with audiovisual equipment.
   b. Our company is the leading distributor of electronic equipment.
   c. We need no introduction.

3. **Action**
   a. Would you please send me a copy of your latest price list?
   b. If possible, I would like to have your catalog.
   c. Send me something, please.

4. **Closing**
   a. I appreciate your prompt attention to my request.
   b. Could you send it quickly?
   c. Thank you in advance for sending the brochures.

That's *Good* **Business!**

Look at the e-mail on page 51. The e-mail address includes the letters *pe* at the end. These letters are called a country code. The letters *pe* mean *Peru*. Some e-mail addresses have country codes and some do not.

Prepositions of Place

Prepositions of place tell *where* you heard about something. *In* is used for print sources, such as newspapers, journals, and magazines. *On* is used for all other media sources, such as radio, TV, and the Internet.

My colleagues and I read the announcement *in* the March 17 *Boston Daily News*.

I heard with interest your commercial *on* radio station WRTG.

Practice 2 Complete these sentences. Use the prepositions *in* or *on*.

1. I read _____ the April 3rd *New York Journal* about your new computer, the Magna PC.

2. My manager saw a report _____ CNN that your new model is being introduced this month.

3. _____ the January issue of *Asia Globe*, I learned that you have developed a new laser printer.

4. I would like more information about the cellular phone listed _____ your spring catalog.

5. We heard about your software, Add Up, _____ *Cable News Today*.

6. I saw an article about your company _____ the Internet.

Sentence Fragments

All sentences in a letter must be complete sentences. A sentence fragment is a sentence that is not complete.

There are three types of sentence fragments.

Missing a noun	Is the largest seller of digital cameras in South America.
Missing a verb	Our company the largest seller of digital cameras in South America.
Dependent clause	Which is the largest seller of digital cameras in South America.
Complete sentence	Our company is the largest seller of digital cameras in South America.

Practice 3 Write *S* if the sentence is a complete sentence. Write *F* if the sentence is a fragment. Rewrite the fragments to make sentences.

1. _F_ Our company the leading producer of computer keyboards.
   Our company is the leading producer of computer keyboards.

2. ____ For the last ten years, we have had over 50 percent of the market.

3. _____ Our main office and its branches, which are located on every continent, can your company promote its products.

_____

_____

4. _____ Since 1959, have been the major supplier of electronic equipment for hospitals.

_____

_____

5. _____ As the largest provider of Internet services, we have put businesses all over the country on the Web.

_____

_____

Requests

In business letters, you must always be polite. You should make requests rather than give commands.

Command	*Have* your sales representative call me.
Request	*I would appreciate* having your sales representative call me.
Command	*Tell* me about your camera.
Request	*Would you please* tell me more about your camera?

Here are some suggestions used in polite requests:

Could you possibly . . .	If it isn't too much trouble . . .	May I ask you to . . .
I would appreciate it if you would/could . . .	If possible, would/could you . . .	Would/could you please . . .
I would be grateful if you would/could . . .	If you have the time . . .	Would/could you possibly . . .

Practice 4   Rewrite these commands as polite requests. Use a different expression for each sentence.

1. Send me a brochure about your new camera.

   If possible, could you send me a brochure about your new camera?

2. Give me your most current prices.

   _____

3. Have your sales representative call me.

   _____

4. Tell me when the product is available.

   _____

5. Fax me a list of distributors.

   _____

Complete the sentences in this letter. Use the words below.

appreciate	custom	known	received
continued	earliest	possible	reference

PIAZZA DELLA REPUBLICA, 17
20124 MILANO
ITALY

TEL: (02) 777098   FAX: (02) 753899

December 1, 20—

Jouris Knockaert
Memphis Design
Tulpplein 4
1018 GX Amsterdam
Netherlands

Dear Mr. Knockaert:

I (1) _____ your spring catalog and was pleased to see you are again making your line of Memphis furniture. As you know, our furniture store is (2) _____ in Europe as the biggest distributor of original Memphis designs.

We would like to carry your new line of Memphis furniture, but we do not want to confuse our customers. Many of our customers will only buy the "original" Memphis furniture from the 1980s. Is the date of manufacture noted on the furniture? If not, would it be (3) _____ to do so?

Your catalog does not make any (4) _____ to custom orders. Our customers often want specific colors of fabric and wood. Is it possible to (5) _____ order these?

I would (6) _____ hearing from you at your (7) _____ convenience and look forward to (8) _____ good relations with Memphis Design.

Sincerely,

R. Caracciolo

R. Caracciolo
Senior Partner

Marian Chu sent a letter requesting information. The shaded boxes show ten places where she made errors. Write the correct word or punctuation above the errors.

WIRELESS ACCESSORIES

BUILDING 2-A, FLOOR 3

WALLAND INDUSTRIAL PARK

WALLAND, TN 37886

(1) April 13 ; 20—

Mr. Lester Freed
Metia Mobile Technology
Michelin House
81 Fulham Road
London, SW3 6RD
United Kingdom

(2) Dearest Mr. Freed:

(3), (4) I read on the Abril issue of the trade journal, *Cellular Today*, about your

(5) new cell phone, the Metia 9444. As we is the major distributor of wireless

(6) accessories on the Internet, the 9444 is of great interest to we .

(7) We would be interesting in selling the batteries, chargers, speakers, and

other accessories that accompany the 9444.

(8) Would you please send at my attention the accessories that will accompany

(9) the 9444 and the proposed list prices? I could appreciate the opportunity to

(10) meet with a sales representative to discussing volume discounts.

I look forward to hearing from you at your earliest convenience.

Sincerely yours,

Marian Chu

Marian Chu
Product Manager

Pretend that you are a major distributor of one of the following products. On a separate piece of paper, write a letter requesting more information about the product.

Source	March 15 *Photo Journal*	Web site
Company	Click Camera Company	Metia Mobile Technology
Product	digital video camera	satellite phone
Model	EZ-Con	GBX 14
Availability	summer	now
Features	PC connection	weight?
	5 hours of video	dimensions?
	JPEG compression	
	self-timer?	
	type of batteries used?	
Price	?	$1,348.95
Sales discount	?	?
Promotional information	?	?
Sales contact info	local sales representative	Ms. Jean Chin

Words and Expressions to Know

Look at this list of words and expressions that were used in the unit. Their definitions are in the glossary at the end of the book.

accessory	distributor	option	ship
brochure	on the market	set apart	source
carry			

UNIT 8 Providing Information

When you send a letter providing information to customers, be sure to answer their specific questions. After you answer the questions, give the customer additional information about your company and its products and services.

Before you write the letter, make sure you are giving the right information to the right person. You may be answering many requests at the same time, and not all customers have the same needs.

GETTING STARTED

1. Read the e-mails between two customer service representatives at Click Camera Company. Note that different companies are requesting different information and services.
2. Complete the Customer Service Checklist.

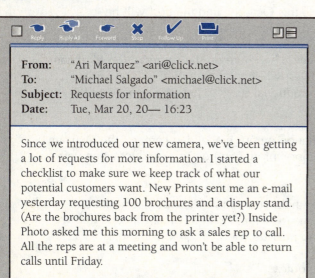

From: "Ari Marquez" <ari@click.net>
To: "Michael Salgado" <michael@click.net>
Subject: Requests for information
Date: Tue, Mar 20, 20— 16:23

Since we introduced our new camera, we've been getting a lot of requests for more information. I started a checklist to make sure we keep track of what our potential customers want. New Prints sent me an e-mail yesterday requesting 100 brochures and a display stand. (Are the brochures back from the printer yet?) Inside Photo asked me this morning to ask a sales rep to call. All the reps are at a meeting and won't be able to return calls until Friday.

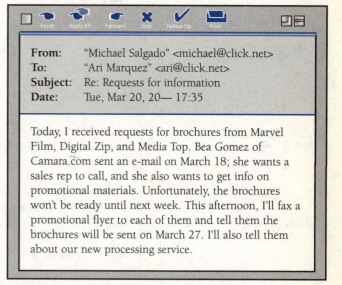

From: "Michael Salgado" <michael@click.net>
To: "Ari Marquez" <ari@click.net>
Subject: Re: Requests for information
Date: Tue, Mar 20, 20— 17:35

Today, I received requests for brochures from Marvel Film, Digital Zip, and Media Top. Bea Gomez of Camara.com sent an e-mail on March 18; she wants a sales rep to call, and she also wants to get info on promotional materials. Unfortunately, the brochures won't be ready until next week. This afternoon, I'll fax a promotional flyer to each of them and tell them the brochures will be sent on March 27. I'll also tell them about our new processing service.

CUSTOMER SERVICE CHECKLIST			
Client	Brochures Requested/Sent	Promotional materials Requested/Sent	Call from sales rep Requested/Made
New Prints	(1) _____	(6) _____	(12) _____
Inside Photo	(2) _____	(7) _____	Mar 20 / Mar 23
Marvel Film	Mar 20 / Mar 27	(8) _____	(13) _____
Digital Zip	(3) _____	(9) _____	(14) _____
Media Top	(4) _____	(10) _____	(15) _____
Camara.com	(5) _____	(11) _____	(16) _____

Look at the different elements of a fax providing information.

FAX

To:	Bea Gomez, New Products Department, Camara.com
From:	Michael Salgado, Customer Service Department, Click Camera
Subject:	The XL-Lite digital camera
Date:	March 20, 20—
Pages:	1
Message	

Dear Ms. Gomez:

Opening

Thank you for your e-mail of March 18 expressing interest in Click Camera's new digital camera, the XL-Lite.

The camera will be available this October, and the cost will be approximately three hundred and fifty dollars ($350.00).

Focus

I will be forwarding next week a brochure on the camera. Jim Markham, one of our sales representatives, will be in touch with you on Friday, March 23, to discuss the promotional services and discounts we offer our distributors.

Action

I am also forwarding information on our new video camera, the Digicam. Mr. Markham will provide more information on this product when you speak with him.

Closing

If there is anything else I can help you with, please do not hesitate to contact me. Your business means a great deal to Click Camera, and we appreciate the opportunity to provide you with quality cameras.

Again, thank you for your inquiry.

Sincerely yours,

Michael Salgado

Michael Salgado
Customer Service Representative

Useful Language

Thank you for your e-mail of _____.

The _____ will be available _____.

I will be forwarding _____.

We appreciate the opportunity to _____.

Again, thank you for your inquiry.

The body of a fax providing information generally has four parts.

Part	Content	Example
Opening	Acknowledge the initial correspondence.	Thank you for your e-mail of March 18 expressing interest in Click Camera's new digital camera, the XL-Lite.
Focus	Provide the information requested.	The camera will be available this October, and the cost will be approximately three hundred and fifty dollars ($350.00).
		I will be forwarding next week a brochure on the camera. Jim Markham, one of our sales representatives, will be in touch with you on Friday, March 27, to discuss the promotional services and discounts we offer our distributors.
Action	Provide additional information.	I am also forwarding information on our new video camera, the Digicam. Mr. Markham will provide more information on this product when you speak with him.
Closing	Offer additional help and thank them for their inquiry.	If there is anything else I can help you with, please do not hesitate to contact me. Your business means a great deal to Click Camera, and we appreciate the opportunity to provide you with quality cameras.
		Again, thank you for your inquiry.

Practice 1

In each question, two of the sentences are appropriate to use in a letter providing information. Circle the letters of the two sentences.

1. **Opening**
   a. Thank you for your letter of June 3rd inquiring about our new Digicam digital video camera.
   b. We are pleased to have the opportunity to respond to your request for more information on our digital cameras.
   c. This is your last chance to buy a camera that uses film.

2. **Focus**
   a. We wondered why you want a sales representative to call you.
   b. The promotional materials you inquired about will be ready on Friday.
   c. We are sending you, under separate cover, a distribution agreement.

3. **Action**
   a. Part of our expanding product line is a mobile phone that takes and sends photos over the phone lines.
   b. We hope you will continue to take good photos.
   c. I am sending a catalog of software developed for our digital cameras.

4. **Closing**
   a. I look forward to working with you in the future.
   b. I'll call you if we want to sell you a camera.
   c. If I can answer any other questions, please call me on my direct line.

Well SAID

The expression *sent under separate cover* means sent separately. Material that doesn't fit in an envelope with a letter is put in a larger envelope or a box and sent separately. Also people may send material separately because the material isn't ready or because they want to contact the recipient again. The letter tells the recipient that the additional material is coming.

Clarifying Numbers

When you write numbers in a business letter, it is a good idea to spell out the number in words. Spelling out the number helps to clarify the information.

The camera will be available this October, and the cost will be approximately *three hundred and fifty dollars ($350.00)*.

Here are some examples of spelling out numbers in letters.

Quantity	Clarification	Amount	Clarification
5 boxes	five (5) boxes	$6.42	six dollars and forty-two cents ($6.42)
10 gross	ten (10) gross	$3,500	three thousand five hundred dollars ($3,500)

Practice 2

These sentences have unclear information. Ask for clarification. Write out the number first, and follow it with the number in parentheses.

1. Unclear The total is thirty-two dollars ($3.20).

Clarification Is the total thirty-two dollars ($32.00) or _three_ dollars and _twenty_ cents ($3.20)?

2. Unclear We will need six (60) boxes of printer paper.

Clarification Do you want six (_____) boxes of printer paper or sixty (_____) boxes of printer paper?

3. Unclear Please send us one (100) dozen brochures.

Clarification Do you need _____ (_____) dozen brochures or _____ (_____) dozen brochures.

4. Unclear We asked that payment be received no later than 01/02.

Clarification Is payment due by _____ 1st or _____ 2nd?

5. Unclear Please submit the report on the fifteenth of every month (for example, June 5).

Clarification Are reports to be submitted on the _____ (_____) or the _____ (_____) of every month?

6. Unclear I ordered four (40) boxes of envelopes.

Clarification Did you order _____ (_____) or _____ (_____) boxes of envelopes?

Commas with Conjunctions

Use a comma when you combine two sentences with a conjunction (*that, and, or, nor, yet*). The comma always comes before the conjunction.

The camera will be available this October, *and* the cost will be approximately three hundred and fifty dollars ($350.00).

Practice 3   Combine the following sentences into one sentence. Choose the correct conjunction, and use a comma.

1. I am enclosing the price list with this letter. I am forwarding the catalog under separate cover. (**and** / or)

   I am enclosing the price list with this letter, and I am forwarding the catalog under separate cover.

2. A sales representative will e-mail you. She will telephone you. (*yet* / *or*)

   _____

3. We do not have the 999X camera. We have a newer model. (*but* / *nor*)

   _____

4. We appreciate your order. We hope to work with you again. (*or* / *and*)

   _____

5. The brochure is ready now. The camera will be sent next week. (*yet* / *but*)

   _____

Also and In Addition

Use the words *also* and *in addition* when you write about more than one action. These words provide continuity and rhythm in a letter.

Also comes before the action verb. *In addition* usually comes at the beginning of a sentence.

   I am forwarding a brochure.
   I am *also* forwarding information on our new video camera.
   In addition, I am enclosing a list of our distributors.

Practice 4   Write new sentences that provide continuity. Use the words provided.

1. I will be sending you our new brochure when it is available.
   also   *free samples*

   I will also be sending free samples.

2. We are shipping the new cameras this week.
   In addition   *the software*

   _____

3. I look forward to answering any questions you might have.
   In addition   *to working with you in the future*

   _____

4. I am attaching a price list to this letter.
   also   *an order form*

   _____

5. I am enclosing information on the camera you inquired about.
   In addition   *information on our new video camera*

   _____

Complete the sentences in this letter. Use the words below.

addition   hesitate   further   separate
custom-made   inquiry   pleased   your

Memphis Design
Tulpplein 4
1018 GX Amsterdam
Netherlands

December 10, 20—

Mr. Roberto Caracciolo
Design 80
Piazza della Republica, 17
20124 Milano
Italy

Dear Mr. Caracciolo:

Thank you for (1) _____ letter of December 1. We, too, are excited about our line of Memphis furniture reproductions.

I am (2) _____ to tell you that all reproductions are labeled and cannot be confused with the original Memphis furniture we produced in the 1980s. In (3) _____, each reproduction is stamped with the date it was produced.

I am sorry that we cannot fulfill your request for custom orders of fabric or wood at this time. Perhaps we will do this in the future. Our Roma line of fine furniture can be (4) _____. A Roma catalog will be sent to you under (5) _____ cover.

If you have any (6) _____ questions, please do not (7) _____ to contact me directly.

Again, thank you for your (8) _____.

Sincerely yours,

Jouris Knockaert

Jouris Knockaert
President, Memphis Design

Lester Freed sent a letter providing information. The shaded boxes show ten places where he made errors. Write the correct word or punctuation above the errors.

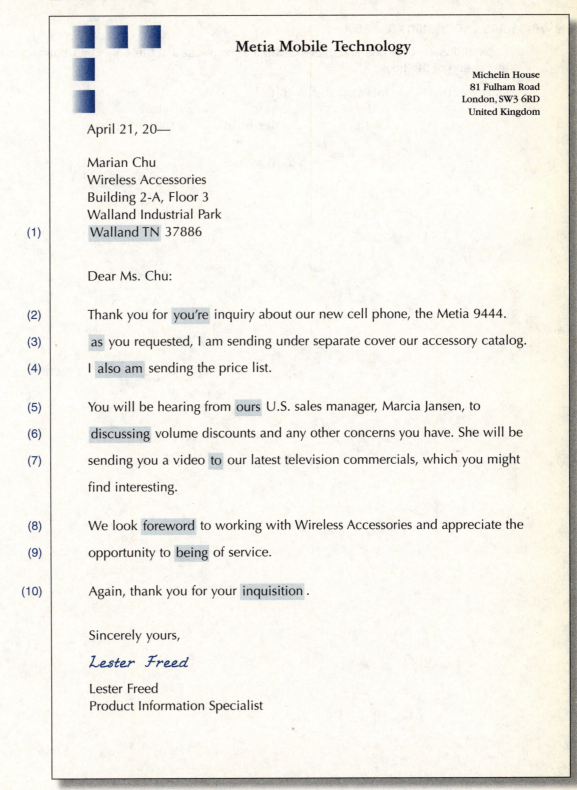

Metia Mobile Technology

Michelin House
81 Fulham Road
London, SW3 6RD
United Kingdom

April 21, 20—

Marian Chu
Wireless Accessories
Building 2-A, Floor 3
Walland Industrial Park
(1) Walland TN 37886

Dear Ms. Chu:

(2) Thank you for you're inquiry about our new cell phone, the Metia 9444.
(3) as you requested, I am sending under separate cover our accessory catalog.
(4) I also am sending the price list.

(5) You will be hearing from ours U.S. sales manager, Marcia Jansen, to
(6) discussing volume discounts and any other concerns you have. She will be
(7) sending you a video to our latest television commercials, which you might
find interesting.

(8) We look foreword to working with Wireless Accessories and appreciate the
(9) opportunity to being of service.

(10) Again, thank you for your inquisition .

Sincerely yours,

Lester Freed

Lester Freed
Product Information Specialist

On a separate piece of paper, reply to the letter that you wrote in Unit 7. Make up the prices, sales discounts, and information about the promotional materials.

Words and Expressions to Know

Look at this list of words and expressions that were used in the unit. Their definitions are in the glossary at the end of the book.

clarification	forward	initial	price list
continuity	fulfill	inquiry	return
flyer	in touch	order form	under separate cover

UNIT 9

Writing Claim Letters

A claim letter is a letter that you write to a company to point out a problem. Some problems that you write about in claim letters include: receiving the wrong products, receiving damaged products, or receiving an incorrect invoice.

Before you write the letter, make sure you have all the information about the problem. If necessary, contact other people in your company. Ask them if they have anything to add.

GETTING STARTED

1. Read the e-mails between two co-workers at Wils & Company, Ltd. They are having problems with several shipments.
2. Complete the Shipments Received Log.

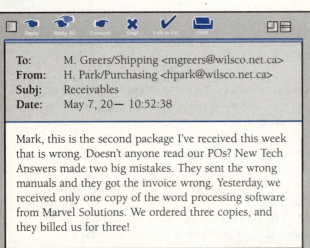

To: M. Greers/Shipping <mgreers@wilsco.net.ca>
From: H. Park/Purchasing <hpark@wilsco.net.ca>
Subj: Receivables
Date: May 7, 20— 10:52:38

Mark, this is the second package I've received this week that is wrong. Doesn't anyone read our POs? New Tech Answers made two big mistakes. They sent the wrong manuals and they got the invoice wrong. Yesterday, we received only one copy of the word processing software from Marvel Solutions. We ordered three copies, and they billed us for three!

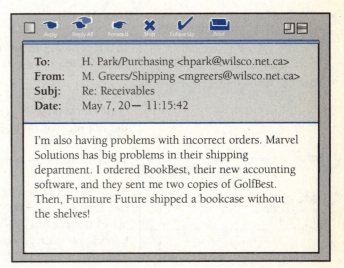

To: H. Park/Purchasing <hpark@wilsco.net.ca>
From: M. Greers/Shipping <mgreers@wilsco.net.ca>
Subj: Re: Receivables
Date: May 7, 20— 11:15:42

I'm also having problems with incorrect orders. Marvel Solutions has big problems in their shipping department. I ordered BookBest, their new accounting software, and they sent me two copies of GolfBest. Then, Furniture Future shipped a bookcase without the shelves!

SHIPMENTS RECEIVED LOG					
Vendor	Ordered	Date (mo./day)	Received	Date (mo./day)	Comments
New Tech Answers	1 Manual TM-0053-3	4/1	2 Manual TM-0035-3	5/7	Invoice received for US$32.50; should be Can$32.50 or US$22.18.
	1 Manual TM-0056-7	4/1			
Marvel Solutions	3 Word processing software	5/2	(1)	(2)	Request they send two more copies of word processing software.
Marvel Solutions	(3)	4/10	(4)	4/14	Return GolfBest; request BookBest.
Furniture Future	(5)	4/11	(6)	(7)	Request they send missing shelves.

Look at the different elements of a claim letter.

Wils & Company, Ltd.

51 Wimbleton Road   Toronto, Ontario M4D 2V8 Canada

TEL: (416) 555-4444 • FAX: (416) 555-4443 • WWW.WILSCO.NET.CA

May 7, 20—

Ms. Rowanda Fisher
Customer Service Manager
New Tech Answers
454 Liberty Road
Philadelphia, PA 19148

Dear Ms. Fisher:

Opening

In a recent shipment from New Tech Answers, there were two problems: we received the wrong manuals and our account was incorrectly billed.

On April 1, we placed the following order: one copy of TM-0053-3 and one copy of TM-0056-7.   On May 7, we received two copies of TM-0035-3.   We did not receive TM-0053-3 or TM-0056-7.

Focus

We are returning—under separate cover—the two copies of TM-0035-3.

Action

Please send us the two (2) manuals that we ordered.   Also, please correct our account, no. 594-NT.   The invoice was for US$32.50 (thirty-two United States dollars and fifty cents).   The correct invoice total should be Can$32.50 (thirty-two Canadian dollars and fifty cents), or, at today's exchange rate, US$22.18 (twenty-two United States dollars and eighteen cents).   A copy of the invoice is enclosed.

Closing

Thank you for your attention to this matter.

Cordially yours,

Holly Park

Holly Park
Purchasing Supervisor

Enclosure: Invoice (photocopy)

Useful Language

In a recent shipment from _____,

On _____ we ordered _____.

On _____ we received _____.

We are returning _____.

Also, please correct _____.

A copy of _____ is enclosed.

The body of a claim letter generally has four parts.

Part	Content	Example
Opening	Explain the problem.	In a recent shipment from New Tech Answers, there were two problems: we received the wrong manuals and our account was incorrectly billed. . . .
Focus	Give your reaction.	We are returning—under separate cover—the two copies of TM-0035-3.
Action	Give a solution.	Please send us the two (2) manuals that we ordered. Also please correct our account, no. 594-NT. . . .
Closing	Thank the reader.	Thank you for your attention to this matter.

Practice 1

In each question, two of the sentences are appropriate to use in a claim letter. Circle the letters of the two sentences.

1. **Opening**
   a. Your shipment of file cabinets arrived damaged on March 12.
   b. We only received two of the three cartons of copy paper that we ordered on April 10.
   c. We would like to receive a catalog.

2. **Focus**
   a. You will receive, by overnight courier, the incorrectly addressed software package.
   b. Thank you for sending the pens, even if they were the wrong color.
   c. I have returned the manuals to your attention.

3. **Action**
   a. I would like you to cancel the order and credit our account for the two manuals we did not receive.
   b. I would like to receive the two additional software packages by November 15.
   c. Your company makes too many mistakes.

4. **Closing**
   a. Don't let it happen again!
   b. Thank you for your attention to this matter.
   c. I appreciate your taking care of this for me.

That's *Good* **Business!**

When you send a claim letter, provide documentation such as receipts, invoices, photos of damaged goods, or anything that would prove there was a problem. Be sure to send photocopies of documentation, not originals. You should keep the originals for your records.

Formal versus Informal Style: Contractions

In business letters, you should always use a formal writing style. One point to remember is that you should not use contractions. Contractions are used in informal or personal correspondence.

Informal   We *didn't* receive TM-0053-3 or TM-0056-7.

Formal   We *did not* receive TM-0053-3 or TM-0056-7.

Informal   We *can't* complete your order because Item 42-A is back ordered.

Formal   We *cannot* complete your order because Item 42-A is back ordered.

Practice 2   Circle the contractions in each sentence. Then rewrite the sentences without using contractions.

1. Please (don't) add shipping and handling to the revised invoice.

   Please do not add shipping and handling to the revised invoice.

2. We're going to send back the incorrect invoice.

   _____

3. We can't approve your shipment.

   _____

4. The order wasn't received by the agreed upon date.

   _____

5. If the item isn't in stock, you may substitute another.

   _____

That's *Good* Business!

When a business letter includes currencies of two or more countries, include the symbol for the countries and their currencies. (See page 67: US$32.50 and Can$32.50.)

Being Concise: Descriptive Adverbs

Business correspondence should be concise. Being concise means that you should use as few words as possible. One way to be concise is to use modifiers, such as descriptive adverbs.

Not concise   Our account was *billed with a lot of different mistakes in it.*

Concise   Our account was *incorrectly billed.*

Practice 3   Rewrite these sentences to make them concise. Use the phrases below.

illegibly written   insufficiently insured   loosely packed
incorrectly added   poorly wrapped

1. The label was written by someone with bad handwriting, which was impossible to read.

   The label was illegibly written.

2. The package was wrapped in a very messy way.

_____

3. The items were all tossed into the box and the wrapping came off.

_____

4. The goods were not insured a sufficient amount to cover damages.

_____

5. The invoice had numbers that didn't add up, and I even used a calculator.

_____

Using Dashes

A dash (—) , or a pair of dashes, can sometimes be used instead of a comma, colon, or parentheses. Dashes can add information, show emphasis, or set off lists.

Add information	We are returning—_under separate cover_—the two copies of TM-0035-3.
Show emphasis	The damaged package—_the one sent by overnight mail_—was refused by the recipient.
Set off lists	The order form containing the information—_date, time, and cost of the shipment_—was delivered by messenger.

Practice 4   Rewrite these sentences using dashes.

1. These manuals (423 and 455) are not the ones we ordered.

These manuals—423 and 445—are not the ones we ordered.

2. Four packages, all from New Media Publishers, were sent to the wrong address.

_____

_____

3. The final order form (the one with so many changes) was difficult to read.

_____

_____

4. The entire contents of the shipment were damaged: bookcases, chairs, and desks.

_____

_____

5. All of the supplies were lost in transit: the books, paper, tape, and disks.

_____

_____

That's Good Business!

If you are having problems over and over again with the same company, you could mention it in the letter. Make sure you are polite, but tell them how you feel. For example, you might say, "Your company always gave us good service in the past, but recently, we've had problems with three orders."

Complete the sentences in this letter. Use the words below.

correct	incorrect	missing	receiving
cover	invoice	order	returning

Wils & Company, Ltd.

51 Wimbleton Road   Toronto, Ontario M4D 2V8 Canada
TEL: (416) 555-4444 • FAX: (416) 555-4443 • WWW.WILSCO.NET.CA

October 20, 20—

Mr. Gerry Kindlet
Telephone Accessories
1746 Park Avenue
New York, NY 10007

Ref: Web order: AF342.56 on October 15, 20—

Dear Mr. Kindlet:

On October 15, we placed an (1) _____ for an Amsta 3245
telephone. We received the following: one telephone without a handset,
a headset we did not order, and an (2) _____ invoice.

I am (3) _____ the headset—under separate
(4) _____ — to you by overnight mail.

Please send the (5) _____ handset. Also, please
(6) _____ the invoice, and send a new one. We did not order a
headset, yet we received one and were charged for two!

I appreciate your making the adjustments to our (7) _____ and
look forward to (8) _____ the handset.

Sincerely yours,

Marian Godal

Marian Godal
Purchasing Department

Lorinda Sanchez sent a claim letter about an incorrect order. The shaded boxes show ten places where she made errors. Write the correct word or punctuation above the errors.

CHEARSLEY TEMP AGENCY
Watts Green
Chearsley
Buckinghamshire HP18 0DD

August 6, 20—

Mr. Murat Ali, President
Ali's Office Furniture
6 Between Towns Road
Oxford OX4 3PP

Dear Mr. Ali:

(1)   We were disappointing to receive your delivery of August 6. None of the items
(2)   where what we ordered.

(3), (4)   We did not sign for the Shipment, and we asked the shipping firm to back take the goods.

(5)   We had ordered the following— one (10) walnut computer desks, three (3) walnut bookcases, and two (2) executive office chairs.

(6)   We are receiving four (4) file cabinets and an oak bookcase without the shelves.

(7), (8), (9)   Maybe someone else received ours furniture? Please sort this out quick, yet send our furniture here as soon as possible.

(10)   Thank you to assisting us with this problem.

Sincerely yours,

Lorinda Sanchez

Lorinda Sanchez
Purchasing Supervisor

Letter Practice 3

Look at the Shipments Received Log you completed on page 67. On a separate piece of paper, write a claim letter to New Tech Answers, Marvel Solutions, or Furniture Future. Look in your local telephone book or on the Internet for addresses to use for the companies.

Words and Expressions to Know

Look at this list of words and expressions that were used in the unit. Their definitions are in the glossary at the end of the book.

account	claim letter	invoice	receive
bill	courier	make an adjustment	shipping and handling
cancel	credit	point out	

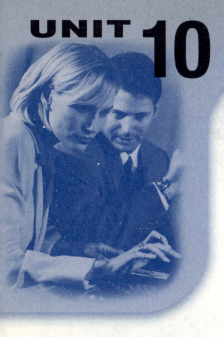

UNIT 10 Writing Adjustment Letters

An adjustment letter is a letter that corrects a mistake. When a company has made a mistake, it is important to acknowledge it, correct it, and apologize for any inconvenience.

Before you write the letter, make sure you have all the information about the situation. If necessary, contact other people in your company. Ask them if they have anything to add. In some cases, you may want to offer something as an apology: a coupon, a discount, or a small gift.

GETTING STARTED

1. Read the e-mails between two executives at New Tech Answers. They have heard complaints about several shipments they have sent.
2. Complete the Adjustment Log.

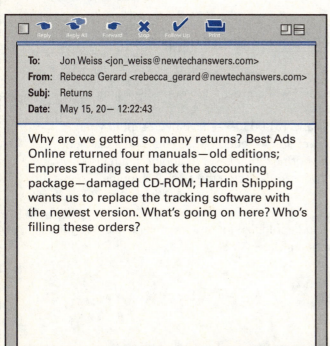

To: Jon Weiss <jon_weiss@newtechanswers.com>
From: Rebecca Gerard <rebecca_gerard@newtechanswers.com>
Subj: Returns
Date: May 15, 20— 12:22:43

Why are we getting so many returns? Best Ads Online returned four manuals—old editions; Empress Trading sent back the accounting package—damaged CD-ROM; Hardin Shipping wants us to replace the tracking software with the newest version. What's going on here? Who's filling these orders?

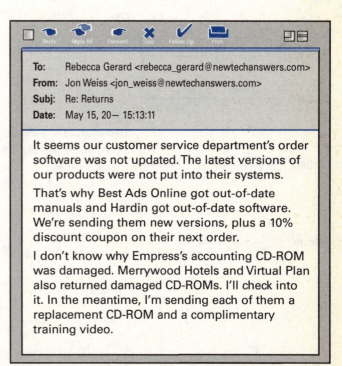

To: Rebecca Gerard <rebecca_gerard@newtechanswers.com>
From: Jon Weiss <jon_weiss@newtechanswers.com>
Subj: Re: Returns
Date: May 15, 20— 15:13:11

It seems our customer service department's order software was not updated. The latest versions of our products were not put into their systems.

That's why Best Ads Online got out-of-date manuals and Hardin got out-of-date software. We're sending them new versions, plus a 10% discount coupon on their next order.

I don't know why Empress's accounting CD-ROM was damaged. Merrywood Hotels and Virtual Plan also returned damaged CD-ROMs. I'll check into it. In the meantime, I'm sending each of them a replacement CD-ROM and a complimentary training video.

ADJUSTMENT LOG					
Client	Best Ads Online	Empress Trading	Hardin Shipping	Merrywood Hotels	(1)
Claim	• old editions of manuals (four) • incorrect invoice	(2)	(3)	damaged accounting CD-ROM	(4)
Adjustment	(5)	(6)	Sent new version with 10% discount	(7)	Sent replacement CD-ROM with a complimentary video coupon

75

Look at the different elements of an adjustment letter.

NEW TECH ANSWERS
454 Liberty Road | Philadelphia, Pennsylvania 19148

May 16, 20—

Ms. Holly Park
Wils & Company, Ltd.
51 Wimbleton Road
Toronto, Ontario M4D 2V8
Canada

Dear Ms. Park:

Opening
We have received your letter of May 7 about the shipment of the wrong manuals.

Focus
We apologize for the error and will correct it to your satisfaction.

Action
Two manuals—TM-0053-3 and TM-0056-7—have been sent to your attention under separate cover. In this letter, I have enclosed a discount coupon for ten percent off your next purchase. In addition, a revised invoice is enclosed. We have also deducted the cost of shipping and handling.

Closing
Again, we regret the error and apologize for any inconvenience. We look forward to serving you in the future.

Sincerely yours,

Rowanda Fisher

Rowanda Fisher
Customer Service Manager

Useful Language

We apologize for the error.

A revised _____ is enclosed.

Again, we regret the error and apologize for any inconvenience.

We look forward to serving you in the future.

The body of an adjustment letter generally has four parts.

Part	Content	Example
Opening	Acknowledge the mistake.	We have received your letter of May 7 about the shipment of the wrong manuals.
Focus	Apologize for the error.	We apologize for the error and will correct it to your satisfaction.
Action	Give a solution.	Two manuals—TM-0053-3 and TM-0056-7—have been sent to your attention under separate cover. . . .
Closing	Apologize again to the reader.	Again, we regret the error and apologize for any inconvenience. We look forward to serving you in the future.

Practice 1   In each question, two of the sentences are appropriate for an adjustment letter. Circle the letters of the two sentences.

1. **Opening**
   a. We have received your March 13th letter regarding the damaged file cabinets.
   b. Thank you for your June 3rd fax detailing the items missing from our shipment.
   c. I'm sorry we don't have any recent catalogs.

2. **Focus**
   a. The post office has been making many mistakes lately.
   b. Please accept our apologies for the inconvenience.
   c. I'm sorry that we did not fill your order to your satisfaction.

3. **Action**
   a. We don't have what you need, so try another company.
   b. The pencils you ordered have been shipped in the color you requested, along with a complimentary pencil sharpener.
   c. You will receive by overnight courier the latest version of the accounting package.

4. **Closing**
   a. Next time, spend more for shipping and this won't happen.
   b. Let me say again how much we regret any inconvenience.
   c. We cannot apologize enough. Your satisfaction is very important to us.

Adjustment Letter Actions

Most adjustment letters have one of these three actions.

refund   The business sends the customer's money back.

replacement The business sends the customer the same item or a similar one in perfect condition.

credit   The business sends the customer a credit to purchase other items that cost the same amount.

These are the three most common actions, but other options are possible. For example, the business could give the customer a choice, or the business could give nothing. Each situation is different.

■ **Practice 2** Write *refund*, *replacement*, or *credit* for each sentence.

1. _*refund*_ You will receive a check for the full amount in the mail.

2. _____ Please return the software package and select another one.

3. _____ Forty-five dollars ($45.00) was credited to your account.

4. _____ The money will be sent to you tomorrow.

5. _____ Please choose another color for your desk.

6. _____ We are out of that particular item, but please select something else from the catalog.

Apologies and Actions

An adjustment letter begins with acknowledging the mistake. Then the writer apologizes, suggests an action, and apologizes again.

First apology We apologize for the error.

Action   Two manuals—TM-0053-3 and TM-0056-7—have been sent to your attention under separate cover. In this letter, I have enclosed a discount coupon for ten percent off your next purchase. In addition, a revised invoice is enclosed. We have also deducted the cost of shipping and handling.

Second apology Again, we regret the error and apologize for any inconvenience.

That's Good Business!

One way that companies apologize for errors is to pay for shipping and handling costs. If the customer already paid their bill, the company can reimburse them. If the company hasn't sent the bill yet, they can deduct the costs before they send the bill.

Practice 3

Write *apology* or *action* for each sentence.

1. __*action*__ You may exchange the item at your convenience.

2. _____ I regret any inconvenience.

3. _____ You will receive a refund for your shipping costs.

4. _____ Please accept this discount coupon.

5. _____ I am sorry that the item you ordered was not in stock.

6. _____ A new fax machine will be sent to you.

Numbers in Sentences

A number that starts a sentence should be spelled out. You can also rewrite the sentence with the number coming later. Review Clarifying Numbers in Unit 8, page 62. Remember that it is sometimes better to use both numbers and words.

Incorrect   *2 manuals* have been sent to your attention.

Correct   *Two manuals—TM-0053-3 and TM 0056-7—have been sent to your attention.*

Two (2) manuals have been sent to your attention.

We have sent *two (2) manuals* to your attention.

Practice 4

Rewrite the following sentences to correct the numbers.

1. $65.00 will be sent to you by check.

   A check for $65.00 will be sent to you. _____ or

   Sixty-five dollars will be sent to you by check. _____ or

   Sixty-five dollars ($65.00) will be sent to you by check.

2. 3 CDs were replaced.

   _____

3. 12 accounting packages have been sent to your attention.

   _____

4. $1,000 will be credited to your account.

   _____

5. 2 manuals have been sent under separate cover.

   _____

6. $80 will be given to you as a store credit.

   _____

That's Good Business!

In an adjustment letter, you do not have to explain why the problem happened. In fact, you should not say anything bad about your company, such as *We've been having problems with our computer system.* Simply apologize and tell the customer that any problem has been fixed.

Complete the sentences in this letter. Use the words below.

apologize   enclosing   providing   regret
damaged   inconvenience   regarding   replacement

NEW TECH ANSWERS

454 Liberty Road | Philadephia, Pennsylvania 19148

May 17, 20—

Ms. Vanessa Idris
Office Manager
Empress Trading Corporation
62504 Putrajaya
Selangor, Malaysia

Dear Ms. Idris:

Thank you for your fax of May 10 **(1)** _____ the damaged
CD-ROM you received. We **(2)** _____ for the damage and for
the **(3)** _____ .

We are shipping by overnight mail a **(4)** _____ CD-ROM.
In addition, we are **(5)** _____ a complimentary training
video. This video will help you make the most of your new
accounting software.

Again, we **(6)** _____ the fact that the accounting software
package arrived with a **(7)** _____ CD-ROM. We are sure
you will find the accounting package useful, and we look forward to
(8) _____ you with other high quality products.

Sincerely yours,

Rowanda Fisher

Rowanda Fisher
Customer Service Manager

Keri Spelling sent an adjustment letter about an incorrect order. She made ten errors. Find the errors, and write the correct word or punctuation above the errors.

Gruenauerstrasse 1
Berlin 12257, Germany

Tel: (49) 30 65 47 90 Fax: (49) 30 65 47 91

(1)   May 16 20—

Ms. Holly Park
Wils & Company, Ltd.
51 Wimbleton Road
Toronto, Ontario M4D 2V8
Canada

Dear Ms. Park:

(2), (3)   Thank you for your May 7 letter. We have receiving the two (12) copies of

(4)   GolfBest you incorrectly were sent. We apologize for the error.

(5)   1 copy of our new accounting software, BookBest, has been sent to you by

(6)   overnight mail as you request.

(7)   Please accept our compliments discount coupon good for ten percent off

future purchases of software from Marvel Solutions.

(8)   Again, we are sorry you were inconveniencing. Our goal is to provide you

(9)   with the highest quality of products or services.

(10)   Sincerely yours:

Keri Spelling

Keri Spelling
Customer Service Department

Letter Practice 3

Look at the adjustment log you completed on page 75. On a separate piece of paper, write an adjustment letter to Best Ads Online, Empress Trading, Hardin Shipping, Merrywood Hotels, or Virtual Plan. Look in your local telephone book or on the Internet for addresses to use in your letter.

Words and Expressions to Know

Look at this list of words and expressions that were used in the unit. Their definitions are in the glossary at the end of the book.

adjustment letter	attention	credit	good for	refund
apology	complimentary	customer service	make the most of	satisfaction

UNIT 11 Writing Reminder Letters and Collection Letters

A reminder letter is a letter that asks if a client has forgotten to pay a bill. It gently reminds clients that they owe payment to a company. If the client does not send payment, the company sends a collection letter. A collection letter is a letter that asks for a late payment (a *collection*) from a client. Both reminder letters and collection letters must be clear and firm, but also polite and professional.

Before you write the letter, make sure you have all the information about the problem. If necessary, contact other people in your company. Ask them if they have anything to add.

GETTING STARTED

1. Read the e-mails between two co-workers at Santrak Industries. They are waiting for several late payments.
2. Complete the Collection Chart. Write the date a check was received or a letter was sent. Write *n/a* (not applicable) if a letter did not need to be sent. Write *?* if the information is not given.

Date: August 18, 20— 11:33:40
To: scaffey@santrak.com
From: jwiley@santrak.com
Subject: Maltech payment

Safiah—

Check receivables. See if we received payment from Gornan Industries. I think they're two months behind payment.

I received the check from Maltech this morning for July's invoice.

Also, Teladyne delivered payment for their last invoice on July 4.

Have other reminders gone out?

J.

Date: August 18, 20— 15:56:11
To: jwiley@santrak.com
From: scaffey@santrak.com
Subject: Maltech payment

Jacob,

Gornan hasn't paid the current invoice. They paid their May invoice on June 30.

Maltech, however, did not pay May's bill. I sent them a second notice on July 15.

I sent AB Alliance several reminders. For their May invoice, I sent reminders on June 30 and July 15. For June, I sent a reminder on July 31. What next?

S.

COLLECTION CHART			
Client	**Invoice(s) sent**	**Check received**	**Reminder/ Collection sent**
Gornan Ind.	May 30	(1) _____	(2) _____
	June 30	(3) _____	(4) _____
	July 30	(5) _____	(6) _____
Maltech	May 30	(7) _____	(8) _____
	July 1	(9) _____	(10) _____
PTD Group	May 15	6/12	(11) _____
	June 15	7/12	(12) _____
AB Alliance Ltd.	May 1	(13) _____	(14) _____
	June 1	(15) _____	(16) _____
	July 1	(17) _____	(18) _____
Aberanderal	May 30	7/2	(19) _____
Teladyne	May 15	5/27	(20) _____
	June 15	(21) _____	(22) _____

83

Look at the different elements of a reminder letter or collection letter.

SANTRAK INDUSTRIES
46B, PAMUR 3/98
88320 PETALING JAYA
SELANGOR, MALAYSIA

August 20, 20—

Mr. Kamur Lana
Accountant
Maltech Medical Equipment
90088 Analayar Road
Selangor, Malaysia

Dear Mr. Lana:

Opening → Your account balance of $2,456 for the invoice dated May 30 was due on June 30.

Focus → All payments are due, in full, within 30 days of receiving an invoice.

Action → Please remit payment no later than August 31.

Closing → We look forward to continuing our valuable relationship with Maltech.

Sincerely yours,

Safiah Caffey

Safiah Caffey
Accountant

Useful Language

Your account balance of _____ was due _____.

All payments are due, in full, _____.

Please remit payment _____.

We look forward to continuing our valuable relationship with _____.

The body of a reminder letter or collection letter generally has four parts.

Part	Content	Example
Opening	Identify the missing payment(s).	Your account balance of $2,456 for the invoice dated May 30 was due on June 30.
Focus	Give details about payment.	All payments are due, in full, within 30 days of receiving an invoice.
Action	Review future action.	Please remit payment no later than August 31.
Closing	Be positive about the business relationship.	We look forward to continuing our valuable relationship with Maltech.

Practice 1

In each question, two of the sentences are appropriate to use in a reminder letter or collection letter. Circle the letters of the two sentences.

1. **Opening**
   a. Our invoice of February 28, for $777.56, has not been paid yet.
   b. We have not yet received payment on invoice #445-98 for the sum of $1,223.40.
   c. It is time for you to pay us.

2. **Focus**
   a. Payment was due by September 30.
   b. We find it hard to believe that you haven't paid yet.
   c. As we agreed, your credit of $450 cannot be applied against this invoice.

3. **Action**
   a. If you would like to discuss terms of payment, please call me.
   b. Please send the full payment by October 31.
   c. Your financial difficulties are not our problem.

4. **Closing**
   a. Our invoice of October 6th, for $233.11, has not been paid yet.
   b. If you do not pay immediately, we will forward this claim to a collection agency.
   c. We look forward to receiving payment immediately.

That's
Good Business!

A collection agency is a company that finds people who owe money to another business and forces them to pay it. It is best to make payments to the original business where you owe money before that business sends your account to a collection agency.

Time Expressions

Well SAID

In all business letters, including reminder and collection letters, it is important to be polite and professional. All clients are important, including clients who pay late.

The time expressions *no later than, by, on,* and *within* are close in meaning. It is important to use the correct expression so readers understand what they have to do. Look at the explanations below.

> *No later than* August 31 means payment can be received at any time but must be received by that specific date.
>
> *By August 31* means payment can be received at any time but must be received by that specific date.
>
> *On August 31* means payment is due on that specific date.
>
> *Within* the month of August means payment can be received any time during that month but must be received before the month ends.

Practice 2 Choose the words that best complete the sentences.

1. We expect payment *by / within* May 31.
2. Invoices are sent *on / no later than* 14 days after we ship the order.
3. The check should be there *on / within* the week.
4. We will turn this matter over to a collection agency *on / within* March 3rd if we have not heard from you.
5. Please contact me *by / on* the end of the week to discuss this matter.
6. We sent your first invoice *by / on* April 22nd.

Articles

The words *the, a,* and *an* are articles. Use *the* to refer to something specific; use *a* and *an* to refer to something general or unknown.

> Your account balance of $2,456 for *the* invoice dated May 30 was due on June 30.
>
> All payments are due, in full, within 30 days of receiving *an* invoice.

Practice 3 Choose the articles that best complete the sentences.

1. This is *a / the* fourth reminder we have sent.
2. *An / The* amount of $5,699 is still due on this account.
3. We look forward to serving you in *a / the* future.
4. We received *an / the* empty envelope from your accounting department.
5. We must receive payment by the end of *a / the* week.
6. At this point, *a / the* partial payment would be better than no payment at all.

Look forward to + gerund

Use the expression *look forward to* followed by a gerund [*-ing* verb functioning as a noun] to talk about something positive that will happen in the future. Do not use an infinitive or other verb form. You may also use a noun that is not a gerund.

Incorrect	Infinitive	We look forward *to continue* our valuable relationship with Maltech.
	Other verb form	We look forward to *continued* our valuable relationship with Maltech.
Correct	Gerund	We look forward to *continuing* our valuable relationship with Maltech.
	Other noun	We look forward to *our next project* with Maltech.

Practice 4   Rewrite these incorrect sentences using the expression *look forward to* + gerund.

1. We look forward to receive payment immediately.

   We look forward to receiving payment immediately.

2. I look forward to hear from you about this issue.

   _____

3. Singalay looks forward to serves you in the future.

   _____

4. I look forward to discuss a payment plan that will work for both of us.

   _____

5. We look forward to continue our relationship with Gornan Industries.

   _____

6. I look forward to knew your thoughts on this topic.

   _____

That's Good Business!

Many companies send a second invoice before they send a collection letter. Often you have to send more than one collection letter before a client sends payment. Each new letter that you send about a late payment should be firmer than the last.

Complete the sentences in this letter. Use the words below.

Accountant   credit   in full   payment
balance   due   invoice   reminder

TYMAN CONSTRUCTION
730 Las Flores Road
Palm Coast, Florida 32142

October 30, 20—

Ms. Lorena Keeler
P.O. Box 921197
Palm Coast, FL 32142-1197

Dear Ms. Keeler:

Your account (1) _____ of $136.99 for (2) _____
number 1990-321 was (3) _____ on September 4.

All accounts are due, (4) _____, within 30 days.

This is your second (5) _____. Please remit
(6) _____ immediately.

We hope to help you maintain your excellent (7) _____ with
Tyman Construction.

Sincerely yours,

Abdul Aziz

Abdul Aziz

(8) _____

Alejandro Comar sent a collection letter about a late payment. He made ten errors. Find the errors, and write the correct word or punctuation above.

ABLAR

Zona E, Hangar 7
15230 México D.F.
México

December 12, 20—

Mr. Samuel Augustine
Basada Steel Traders
5 State Entry Road
New Delhi 110056
India

Dear Mr. Augustine:

(1), (2) A balance of $1,456 for invoice number 4334-50 was due within June 30.

(3) As you know, all accounts are dues within 30 days.

(4) This is a fifth reminder that we have sent you regarding this invoice.

(5) However, we have not receiving payment or any communication from you about this matter.

(6) At this point, we regret that we must turn over this claim to the collection

(7) agency. This agency will contact you on the end of the month.

(8), (9) We know you are the valued client, and we look forward to settle this account immediately.

(10) Goodbye,

Alejandro Comar

Alejandro Comar
Senior Accountant

On a separate piece of paper, write a letter to Gornan Industries or Maltech. Use the information in the chart below.

1. Write a collection letter to Gornan Industries about the June 30 invoice.
2. Write a collection letter to Maltech about the May 30 invoice.

Client	Invoice(s) sent	Check rec'd	Reminder sent
Gornan Ind.	May 30	June 30	
	June 30		
	July 30		
Maltech	May 30		July 15
	July 1	August 18	

Words and Expressions to Know

Look at this list of words and expressions that were used in the unit. Their definitions are in the glossary at the end of the book.

collection agency   headquarters   partial   remit
firm   notice   reminder

Replying to Reminder Letters and Collection Letters

When you receive a reminder letter or a collection letter, you must reply quickly. Your reply letter should explain the situation. Remember that your business's reputation is very important.

Before you write the letter, make sure you have all the information about the problem. If necessary, contact other people in your company. Ask them if they have anything to add. Check that all of the invoice numbers, amounts, and dates are correct before you send the letter.

GETTING STARTED

1. Read the e-mails between two co-workers at Maltech Medical Equipment. They have to reply to one of their vendors about a late payment.
2. Complete the Accounting Log.

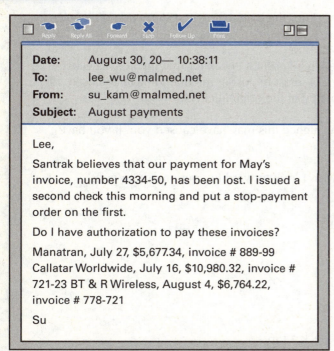

Date: August 30, 20— 10:38:11
To: lee_wu@malmed.net
From: su_kam@malmed.net
Subject: August payments

Lee,

Santrak believes that our payment for May's invoice, number 4334-50, has been lost. I issued a second check this morning and put a stop-payment order on the first.

Do I have authorization to pay these invoices?

Manatran, July 27, $5,677.34, invoice # 889-99
Callatar Worldwide, July 16, $10,980.32, invoice # 721-23 BT & R Wireless, August 4, $6,764.22, invoice # 778-721

Su

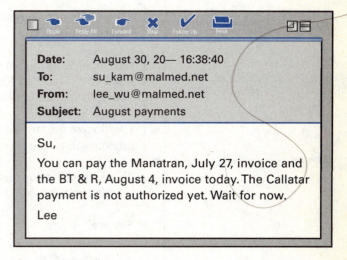

Date: August 30, 20— 16:38:40
To: su_kam@malmed.net
From: lee_wu@malmed.net
Subject: August payments

Su,

You can pay the Manatran, July 27, invoice and the BT & R, August 4, invoice today. The Callatar payment is not authorized yet. Wait for now.

Lee

ACCOUNTING LOG				
Invoice no.	Amount	Date	Vendor	Paid
345-339	$126.78	August 16	ABR Steel	August 14
889-99	(1) _____	July 27	Manatran	(2) _____
(3) _____	$6764.22	August 4	BT & R Wireless	(4) _____
4334-50	$2,456.00	May 30	Santrak	(5) _____
721-23	$10,980.32	July 16	(6) _____	(7) _____

Look at the different elements of a letter replying to a reminder letter or collection letter.

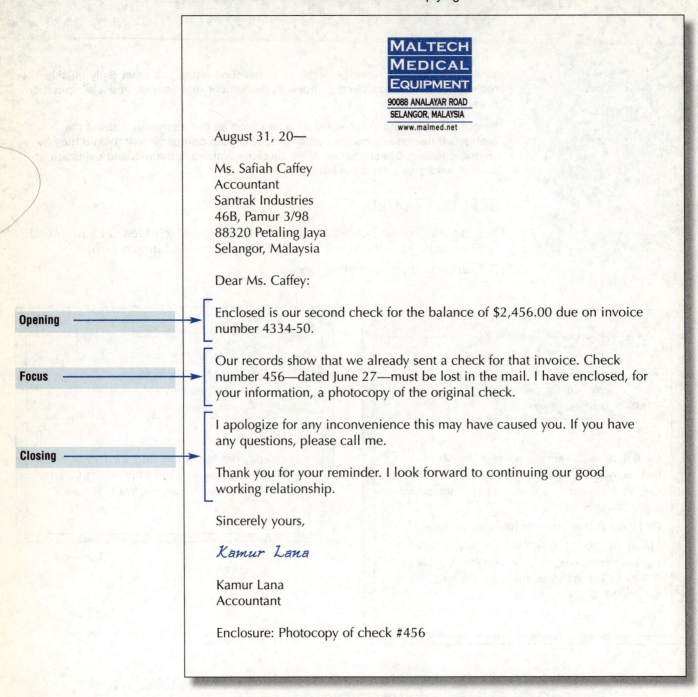

MALTECH MEDICAL EQUIPMENT
90088 ANALAYAR ROAD
SELANGOR, MALAYSIA
www.malmed.net

August 31, 20—

Ms. Safiah Caffey
Accountant
Santrak Industries
46B, Pamur 3/98
88320 Petaling Jaya
Selangor, Malaysia

Dear Ms. Caffey:

Opening

Enclosed is our second check for the balance of $2,456.00 due on invoice number 4334-50.

Focus

Our records show that we already sent a check for that invoice. Check number 456—dated June 27—must be lost in the mail. I have enclosed, for your information, a photocopy of the original check.

Closing

I apologize for any inconvenience this may have caused you. If you have any questions, please call me.

Thank you for your reminder. I look forward to continuing our good working relationship.

Sincerely yours,

Kamur Lana

Kamur Lana
Accountant

Enclosure: Photocopy of check #456

Useful Language

Enclosed is our check for _____.

Our records show _____.

I have enclosed, for your information, _____.

I apologize for any inconvenience this may have caused you.

Thank you for your reminder. I look forward to continuing our good working relationship.

The body of a letter replying to a reminder letter or collection letter generally has three parts.

Part	Content	Example
Opening	Identify the missing payment(s).	Enclosed is our second check for the balance of $2,456.00 due on invoice number 4334-50.
Focus	Give details about payment.	Our records show that we already sent a check for that invoice. Check number 456—dated June 27—must be lost in the mail. I have enclosed, for your information, a photocopy of the original check.
Closing	Apologize for any inconvenience, and thank the reader.	I apologize for any inconvenience this may have caused you. If you have any questions, please call me. Thank you for your reminder. I look forward to continuing our good working relationship.

Practice 1

In each question, two of the sentences are appropriate to use in a letter replying to a reminder letter or collection letter. Circle the letters of the two sentences.

1. **Opening**
   a. We have already paid all of our accounts.
   b. According to our records, your invoice 9980334 was paid in full on March 13.
   c. Please let us know how much we still owe.

2. **Focus**
   a. Our records indicate that our check was returned as "undeliverable."
   b. The check for invoice #450-33 was sent on January 3.
   c. We look forward to doing business with you again in the future.

3. **Closing**
   a. Our first installment was paid last month.
   b. I am sorry for the confusion.
   c. Please call if you have questions.

That's Good Business!

Many businesses keep electronic or hard copies of all transactions. These copies will prove payment was made in case there is a problem. If payment was made, received, and deposited, there will be a cancelled check.

Already, Yet, and Still

The adverbs *already, yet,* and *still* are close in meaning.

Already   Something happened before now.
           Position: midsentence
           Our records show that we *already* sent a check for
           that invoice.

Yet   Something did not happen before now.
           Position: End of sentence
           Our records show that we have not sent a check for that
           invoice *yet*.

Still   A situation continues to exist from the past until now.
           Position: midsentence.
           Our records show that we *still* have not sent a check for
           that invoice.

Practice 2   Complete the following sentences with the correct adverb.

1. The check has _____ been stopped.

2. We have _____ sent the check, so please stop sending notices.

3. We have _____ not received invoice #4434.

4. If you have _____ sent payment, please disregard this notice.

5. Our accounting department has not located your check _____.

6. We have not determined the cause for this lateness _____.

7. If you _____ feel that we owe on this invoice, please let us know your reasons.

Dates

Most people use one of two styles for writing dates: U.S. or non-U.S.

U.S. style   August 31, 20—
Non-U.S. style   31 August 20—

U.S. style uses a comma after the day when the year is included; non-U.S. style does not use commas.

It is not always necessary to include the year when writing dates. In the model letter, the writer writes about a check dated June 27. The letter was written in August. It is assumed that both dates are in the same year. When you do not include the year, do not use a comma.

The check is dated June 27.

If the reader may be confused, include the year. If your letter is dated in one year and a date from another year is mentioned, always include the year.

February 2, 2004
Dear Mr. O'Leary:
We have not received payment for the invoice dated November 1, 2003.

Practice 3   Correct the dates in the following sentences. Spell out the months.

1. We expect payment no later than 8, 31, 20—. (U.S.) _____
2. Invoice #445-112 was mailed on 3, July, 20—. (Non-U.S.) _____
3. You didn't respond to our first invoice, sent 20—, 14, March. (Non-U.S.) _____
4. Your first installment arrived on 7/17. (U.S.) _____
5. Thank you for your letter of 20—, December 1. (U.S.) _____

Commas with Introductory Phrases

Use a comma to set off an introductory phrase.

Incorrect   *If you have any questions* please call me.
Correct   *If you have any questions,* please call me.

Practice 4   Add commas to these sentences.

1. As you know, it is our policy to pay all accounts immediately.
2. According to our records we have already made this payment.
3. Given the misunderstanding we think it would be fair for you to offer us a discount.
4. Considering the weather problems I understand why your payment is late.
5. After reviewing your letter I'd like to discuss the original costs with you.
6. If you have any questions please do not hesitate to contact me.

Thank you for + noun or gerund

Use the expression *thank you for* followed by a noun or gerund [*-ing* verb functioning as a noun]. Do not use an infinitive or other verb form.

Incorrect	Infinitive	Thank you for *to remind* me.
	Other verb form	Thank you for *reminded* me.
Correct	Noun	Thank you for *your reminder.*
	Gerund	Thank you for *reminding* me.

Practice 5   Rewrite the incorrect sentences using the correct noun or gerund.

1. Thank you for send me a second invoice.

   Thank you for sending me a second invoice. _____

2. Thank you for remind us to pay.

   _____

3. Thank you for your understand about our late payment.

   _____

4. Thank you, in advance, for gave us an extension on this payment.

   _____

5. I want to thank you personally for your patient while we were moving offices.

   _____

Complete the sentences in this letter. Use the words below.

accounts	check	issued	stop
authorization	installments	policy	track

COMPONENTS COMPANY

P.O. BOX 10148
WELLINGTON
NEW ZEALAND

(64 4) 473 3750

February 16, 20—

Ms. Marcia Calhoun
Manager, Purchasing Department
Jali & Sons Ltd.
1 Southgate Avenue
Southbank, Victoria 3006
Australia

Dear Ms. Calhoun:

We received your reminder for payment on invoice #456-0120.

As you know, it is our standard (1) _____ to pay all (2) _____ in full within 14 business days. As I discussed with Margot Kulo, we (3) _____ a (4) _____ for this account just six days after receiving your invoice. However, when we realized that our order had been incorrectly filled, we put a (5) _____ on that payment.

At this point, I will ask for (6) _____ to pay this invoice in (7) _____, which will be paid as the corrected shipments arrive to us.

We appreciate your patience while we (8) _____ the source of the unfortunate confusion.

Sincerely yours,

Melina Hamlin

Melina Hamlin
Accounting Manager

Samuel Augustine sent a reply to a collection letter. He made ten errors. Find the errors, and write the correct word or punctuation above the errors.

Basada | Steel Traders

5 State Entry Road
New Delhi 110056
India

December 23, 20—

Alejandro Comar
ABLAR
Zona E, Hangar 7
15230 México D.F.
México

Dear Mr. Comar:

(1) Thank you for your remind about invoice 4334-50 with $1,456 due.

(2) Enclosed is the full payment. We have not received the original invoice still.

(3), (4) While this was the fifth reminder your December, 12 note was only the second we received.

(5) For our accounting purposes we would like to receive an invoice for this

(6), (7) account. It very would be helpful if you could send this and all future invoice by

(8) e-mail. You can already send end-of-year statements by mail. Please send the

(9) invoice before December 31, .

(10) Thank you for your attend to this matter.

Sincerely yours,

Samuel Augustine

Samuel Augustine
Vice President, International Accounts

On a separate piece of paper, write a letter replying to one of these collection situations. Look in your local telephone book or on the Internet for names and addresses to use in your letter.

July 20, 20—

Dear Ms. O'Keefe:

Please see the attached list of your current invoices. We have not yet received your payment for invoice #28830, dated May 31, 20—.

According to our policy, all accounts are due in full within 30 days.

Please do not hesitate to contact me if you have any questions.

Mei Ling
Accountant

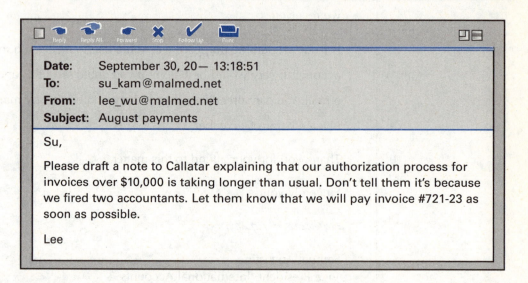

Date: September 30, 20— 13:18:51
To: su_kam@malmed.net
From: lee_wu@malmed.net
Subject: August payments

Su,

Please draft a note to Callatar explaining that our authorization process for invoices over $10,000 is taking longer than usual. Don't tell them it's because we fired two accountants. Let them know that we will pay invoice #721-23 as soon as possible.

Lee

Words and Expressions to Know

Look at this list of words and expressions that were used in the unit. Their definitions are in the glossary at the end of the book.

authorization	installments	paid in full	reputation
confusion	owe	photocopy	unfortunate

UNIT 13 Writing Employee Relations Letters

One common type of business letter is an employee relations letter. There are three main types of employee relations letters: letters of reference, employee announcements, and letters of introduction. These letters describe an employee in an honest and positive way.

Before you write the letter, make sure you have all the facts. These letters are an important source of information about a person, and they must be accurate.

GETTING STARTED

1. Read the e-mails between an executive and his assistant. They discuss several employee relations letters.
2. Complete the Employee Correspondence Checklist. Write a check (✔) if the assistant wrote the letter. Write *To do* if the assistant has not written the letter yet.

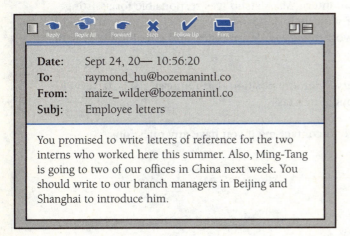

Date: Sept 24, 20— 10:56:20
To: raymond_hu@bozemanintl.co
From: maize_wilder@bozemanintl.co
Subj: Employee letters

You promised to write letters of reference for the two interns who worked here this summer. Also, Ming-Tang is going to two of our offices in China next week. You should write to our branch managers in Beijing and Shanghai to introduce him.

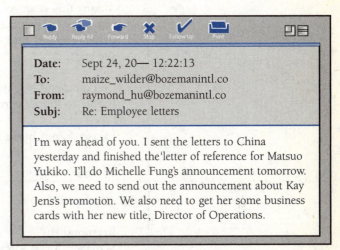

Date: Sept 24, 20— 12:22:13
To: maize_wilder@bozemanintl.co
From: raymond_hu@bozemanintl.co
Subj: Re: Employee letters

I'm way ahead of you. I sent the letters to China yesterday and finished the letter of reference for Matsuo Yukiko. I'll do Michelle Fung's announcement tomorrow. Also, we need to send out the announcement about Kay Jens's promotion. We also need to get her some business cards with her new title, Director of Operations.

EMPLOYEE CORRESPONDENCE CHECKLIST			
Employee	**Reference**	**Announcement**	**Introduction**
Lee Ming-Tang			
Michelle Fung			
Matsuo Yukiko (intern)			
Luis Martinez (intern)			
Kay Jens			

Look at the different elements of a letter of reference.

Bozeman International

6-13-8 Hongo
Bunkyo-ku
Tokyo 181
Japan

September 23, 20—

To whom it may concern:

It is my pleasure to write this letter of reference for Matsuo Yukiko.

Ms. Matsuo was a summer intern at Bozeman International from May to August this year. As an intern, Ms. Matsuo was responsible for assisting our professional staff with their duties. She was efficient, punctual, and detail-oriented. She worked well under pressure and got along well with the staff.

I recommend Ms. Matsuo for any position that requires a self-starter who is able to follow through on a task.

Please do not hesitate to contact me if you have any questions.

Sincerely,

Raymond Hu

Raymond Hu
Manager, Asian Sales

Useful Language

It is my pleasure to write this letter of reference for _____.

_____ was a _____ at [company name] from _____ to _____.

_____ was responsible for _____.

I recommend _____ for _____.

The body of a letter of reference generally has four parts.

Practice 1 Complete the chart using the Model Letter of Reference.

Part	Content	Example
Opening	Introduce the person you are writing about.	It is my pleasure to write this letter of reference for Matsuo Yukiko.
Focus	Give relevant details about the person.	(1) _____ _____ _____ _____ _____ _____
Action	Discuss the future.	(2) _____
Closing	Restate the main idea. Ask the person to contact you if necessary.	(3) _____ _____

Practice 2 Write *O* if the sentence is for the Opening, *F* for Focus, or *A* for Action.

1. _____ Ms. Namazawa handled travel arrangements for seven executives.

2. _____ I am writing this letter on behalf of our employee, Mr. Tam Oshanter, who worked at Silikar Industries from 1998–2001.

3. _____ She has the skills and the energy to succeed in whatever she pursues.

4. _____ Mr. Ko maintained steady sales even when the market was slow.

5. _____ I highly recommend Miss Benoit as a graphic designer.

6. _____ Mr. Fu will surely become a leader in our region's fight to save the environment.

7. _____ This serves as a letter of reference for Maya Eng, my former assistant.

8. _____ Ms. Belka has my recommendation as a reliable, trustworthy employee.

Well SAID

In China, Japan, and Korea, the family name comes first, so *Matsuo Yukiko* is *Ms. Matsuo*. However, when a person uses an English first name, Western order is used, as in *Raymond Hu*.

Adjectives and Adverbs

Letters of reference describe employees and how they work. These letters often contain many adjectives and adverbs. Remember that adjectives describe nouns, and adverbs describe verbs.

Incorrect	She was *efficiently*.
	She completed her projects very *accurate*.
Correct	She was *efficient*.
	She completed her projects very *accurately*.

Practice 3   Choose the correct adjectives or adverbs to complete the sentences.

1. Ms. Matsuo performed all of her duties *professional / professionally*.

2. She was *efficient / efficiently* in preparing and mailing correspondence.

3. He types quickly and *accurate / accurately*.

4. Miss Wei designed an *attractive / attractively* brochure for a major client.

5. He communicates *effective / effectively* with both clients and co-workers.

6. All of her projects were on schedule because her documentation was always *complete / completely*.

7. I *high / highly* recommend Mr. King for any engineering position.

8. Mr. Cho is very *honest / honestly* and loyal.

9. I will be *happy / happily* to answer any questions about Ms. Stein.

10. He had *full / fully* responsibility for the department's budget.

That's Good Business!

There are two types of reference letters. In one type, you reply to a specific request to recommend someone for a job. In the other type, you write a general recommendation that can be used in more than one situation.

Look at the different elements of an employee announcement.

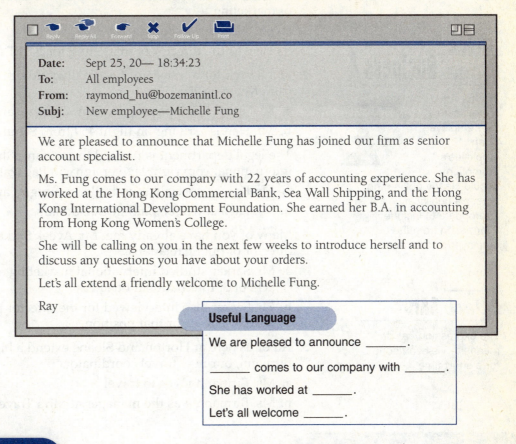

Date: Sept 25, 20— 18:34:23
To: All employees
From: raymond_hu@bozemanintl.co
Subj: New employee—Michelle Fung

We are pleased to announce that Michelle Fung has joined our firm as senior account specialist.

Ms. Fung comes to our company with 22 years of accounting experience. She has worked at the Hong Kong Commercial Bank, Sea Wall Shipping, and the Hong Kong International Development Foundation. She earned her B.A. in accounting from Hong Kong Women's College.

She will be calling on you in the next few weeks to introduce herself and to discuss any questions you have about your orders.

Let's all extend a friendly welcome to Michelle Fung.

Ray

Useful Language

We are pleased to announce _____.

_____ comes to our company with _____.

She has worked at _____.

Let's all welcome _____.

Composing Your Message

The body of an employee announcement generally has four parts.

Practice 4   Complete the chart using the Model E-Mail: Employee Announcement.

Part	Content	Example
Opening	Introduce the person you are writing about.	(1) _____
Focus	Give relevant details about the person.	Ms. Fung comes to our company with 22 years of accounting experience. She has worked at the Hong Kong Commercial Bank, Sea Wall Shipping, and the Hong Kong International Development Foundation. . . .
Action	Discuss the future.	(2) _____
Closing	Restate the main idea.	(3) _____

Read these opening sentences for letters announcing a new employee. Then circle the letter of the sentence that gives a relevant detail about the employee.

1. We are pleased to introduce Luis Zambrana, the new director of marketing.
   a. He was born in Bolivia.
   b. He was the director of marketing for BT&T for nine years.

2. Our search for a translator has finally paid off; Han Ki-sun will arrive from Korea on the 19th.
   a. Ki-sun speaks Japanese, Korean, Chinese, and English fluently.
   b. Mr. Han is arriving on flight 459 from Seoul.

3. The legal department is pleased to announce that it has found an international copyright lawyer, Ignacio Pagaza.
   a. Mr. Pagaza specializes in trade, copyright, and patent law.
   b. Mr. Pagaza will be paid in U.S. dollars.

4. Many of you have already met Mr. Aveek Sarkar, our new assistant director of public relations.
   a. Mr. Sarkar studied international marketing at the West Bengal School of International Business.
   b. Mr. Sarkar also interviewed for the director position, but he was too inexperienced for that position.

5. All of us here at Horton and Sloane extend a big welcome to Eva Birmann, our new travel coordinator.
   a. Ms. Birmann loves to travel.
   b. Ms. Birmann was the manager at Mira Travel Services for ten years.

That's Good Business!

A letter announcing a new employee or an employee's promotion should clearly outline the person's qualifications. It is appropriate to include information from the employee's résumé.

Well SAID

The expression *call on* means to visit someone for a short time.

Writing Your Message

The Simple Past and the Present Perfect

When you refer to a specific past time, use the simple past verb form. When you refer to an unspecified past time, use the present perfect verb form. The exact time is not important.

Simple Past	She *worked* at the Hong Kong Commercial Bank from 1984–1992.
Present Perfect	She *has worked* at the Hong Kong Commercial Bank, Sea Wall Shipping, and the Hong Kong International Development Foundation.

■ **Practice 6**

Choose the correct verb form to complete the sentences.

1. He *served / has served* the company well, and we will be sad to see him go.

2. From 2001–2002, Ms. Hui *participated / has participated* in a government-sponsored program researching recent cell phone technology.

3. Ms. Klein *worked / has worked* as the director of design for women's clothes at Husseby's for six years.

4. She *designed / has designed* many award-winning business suits.

5. Mika *won / has won* the prestigious D.A.R. Engineering Award in 1999.

Look at the different elements of a letter of introduction.

Bozeman International

6-13-8 Hongo
Bunkyo-ku
Tokyo 181
Japan

September 23, 20—

Mr. Charles H. C. Kao
Sedder, Kao and Tang, Ltd.
Henderson Centre
22 Wenjin Street
Beijing 100005
People's Republic of China

Dear Charles,

This letter will introduce Lee Ming-Tang, our sales manager, who will be in your city October 12–14 scouting new leads. I know this is a busy time for you, but I hope you will be able to meet with him.

Ming-Tang has been with our company for ten years and has rapidly moved up from a regional sales position to manager of our sales division. He not only is hard working but also is a great golfer. I know you two will have a lot in common.

If you have any leads he might pursue or suggestions about contacts in your area, I'm sure he would be glad to hear them.

Thank you in advance for meeting with Ming-Tang. I look forward to seeing you soon.

Yours,

Ray

Raymond Hu
Manager, Asian Sales

Useful Language

This letter will introduce _____.

I hope you will be able to meet with _____.

_____ has been with our company for _____ years and has _____.

Thank you in advance for meeting with _____.

The body of a letter of introduction generally has four parts.

Practice 7   Complete the chart using the Model Letter of Introduction.

Part	Content	Example
Opening	Introduce the person you are writing about.	(1) _____ _____ _____ _____
Focus	Give relevant details about the person.	(2) _____ _____ _____ _____
Action	Discuss the future.	If you have any leads he might pursue or suggestions about contacts in your area, I'm sure he would be glad to hear them.
Closing	Restate the main idea.	(3) _____ _____

That's Good Business!

A letter of introduction explains why you are introducing the person. Readers need to know how the new person may help them or their business.

Practice 8   Read these opening sentences for letters of introduction. Then circle the letter of the closing sentence that best restates the main idea.

1. My assistant, Roberta Kuo, will be in Hong Kong next week to meet with all of the branch managers.

   a. Ms. Kuo looks forward to meeting you in person.

   b. Ms. Kuo has been working for me for ten years now.

2. Mr. Sukpum hopes to tour both of your production facilities in Thailand when he is there next month.

   a. Thailand is a possible location for our fifth production facility.

   b. Thank you for arranging his tour of your plant.

3. Anna Lewis will speak to your department about her success in moving from a local to a national marketing campaign.

   a. I know that Ms. Lewis's speech will be both enjoyable and informative.

   b. Ms. Lewis has been a great asset to our marketing department.

4. This letter will introduce our new technology manager, Chang Chul-Hi, who will be calling you with questions about your technology needs.

   a. I appreciate your taking the time to answer Mr. Chang's questions.

   b. As you know, we searched for a technology manager for months before promoting Mr. Chang.

5. Our human relations director will be speaking on the importance of multilingualism in new employees.

   a. Her speech will begin at 3:00. I look forward to seeing you there.

   b. Have you considered studying another language?

6. Thank you for agreeing to meet with my uncle when he is in Malaysia.

   a. My uncle is looking forward to your afternoon together.

   b. My uncle met his wife while he was stationed there.

That's Good Business!

In a letter of introduction, it may be appropriate to give personal information about the person if it is directly relevant to the reader.

Not only . . . but also

The expression *not only . . . but also* emphasizes that more than one item is related to a topic. *Not only . . .* and *. . . but also* are placed directly before the parallel elements they join in the sentence.

He *not only* <u>is</u> hard working *but also* <u>is</u> a great golfer.
[verb]   [verb]

Practice 9   Combine the sentences using the expression *not only . . . but also*.

1. She is outgoing and energetic. She is one of the friendliest people I know.

   She not only is outgoing and energetic but also is one of the friendliest people I know.

2. He designed the new product. He designed the marketing slogan.

   _____

   _____

3. Allen is a fair manager. Allen is a caring manager.

   _____

   _____

4. She works harder than anyone I've ever met. She plays golf with complete devotion.

   _____

   _____

5. He would like to tour your main offices. He would like to see your production facility.

   _____

   _____

6. You will enjoy meeting each other. You will have a lot in common.

   _____

   _____

That's Good Business!

In the model letter on page 105, the writer (Ray) uses the first name of the person he is introducing (Ming-Tang). When he signs the letter, he uses only his first name. Ray has known Ming-Tang and the reader of the letter for a long time and has worked closely with them.

Well **SAID**

Don't forget to say *please* and *thank you* when asking a favor.

On a separate piece of paper, write an employee relations letters for one of the following situations.

1. Write a letter of reference for one of your co-workers or classmates. Use real descriptions and specific examples of his or her work and work habits. (You don't have to use his or her real name.)

2. Write an e-mail announcing a new employee. The new employee is you. Use information about yourself in the e-mail.

Words and Expressions to Know

Look at this list of words and expressions that were used in the unit. Their definitions are in the glossary at the end of the book.

branch	employee relations	letter of introduction	under pressure
contact	extend	letter of reference	unspecified
employee announcement	follow through	reliable	

Writing Customer Relations Letters

A customer relations letter helps to build and maintain a good relationship between a business and its customers. A customer relations letter can announce many different topics, such as a new address, a product promotion, or a product recall.

Before you write the letter, make sure you have all the facts. Customers need accurate, up-to-date information about the companies they do business with.

GETTING STARTED

1. Read the e-mails between two executives at Electronix International. They discuss several customer relations issues that need to be announced.
2. Complete the Customer Relations Announcements Log.

Date: Jan 07, 20— 09:14:30
To: marie_berger@electronix.com
From: jane_wu@electronix.com
Subject: Recent correspondence

Yesterday, I notified Wiretex One and Coolmail Now that we will be sending replacement phones for the ones we recalled. I'll do MediaGreen and Fonefax 1 today, and Telezip and ChatOnline tomorrow.

Also, don't forget—we need a database search for our Asian and European clients. We need to e-mail them about the change of address for our Malaysian office.

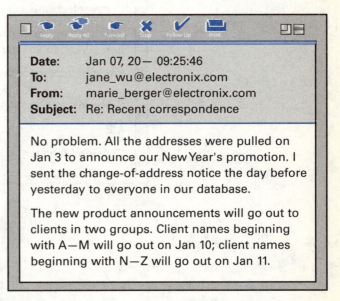

Date: Jan 07, 20— 09:25:46
To: jane_wu@electronix.com
From: marie_berger@electronix.com
Subject: Re: Recent correspondence

No problem. All the addresses were pulled on Jan 3 to announce our New Year's promotion. I sent the change-of-address notice the day before yesterday to everyone in our database.

The new product announcements will go out to clients in two groups. Client names beginning with A—M will go out on Jan 10; client names beginning with N—Z will go out on Jan 11.

CUSTOMER RELATIONS ANNOUNCEMENTS LOG

Client	Change of address	New Year's promotion	Product recall	New products announcement
Wiretex One	(1) _____	(6) _____	(11) _____	Jan 11
Coolmail Now	(2) _____	(7) _____	Jan 6	(16) _____
MediaGreen	(3) _____	(8) _____	(12) _____	(17) _____
Fonefax 1	Jan 5	(9) _____	(13) _____	(18) _____
Telezip	(4) _____	Jan 3	(14) _____	(19) _____
ChatOnline	(5) _____	(10) _____	(15) _____	(20) _____

Look at the different elements of an announcement about a change in a company.

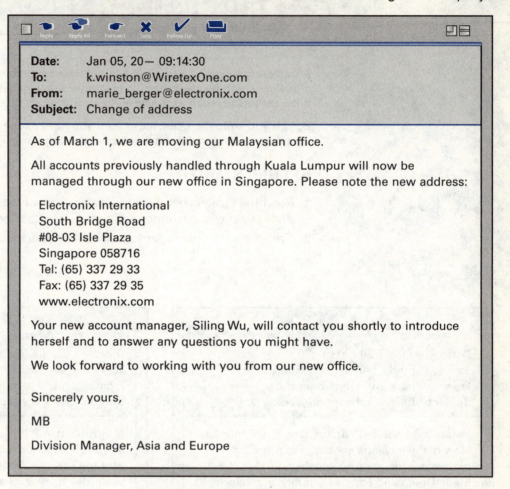

Reply	Reply All	Forward	Stop	Follow Up	Print		

Date: Jan 05, 20— 09:14:30
To: k.winston@WiretexOne.com
From: marie_berger@electronix.com
Subject: Change of address

As of March 1, we are moving our Malaysian office.

All accounts previously handled through Kuala Lumpur will now be managed through our new office in Singapore. Please note the new address:

Electronix International
South Bridge Road
#08-03 Isle Plaza
Singapore 058716
Tel: (65) 337 29 33
Fax: (65) 337 29 35
www.electronix.com

Your new account manager, Siling Wu, will contact you shortly to introduce herself and to answer any questions you might have.

We look forward to working with you from our new office.

Sincerely yours,

MB

Division Manager, Asia and Europe

Useful Language

As of _____, we are moving _____.

Please note the new address.

_____ will contact you _____.

We look forward to working with you from our new office.

Composing Your Message

The body of an announcement about a change in a company generally has four parts.

Practice 1 Complete the chart using the Model E-Mail: Change in Company (Address).

Part	Content	Example
Opening	Tell why you are writing.	As of March 1, we are moving our Malaysian office.
Focus	Give details.	(1) _____ _____ _____
Action	Tell what will happen.	(2) _____ _____ _____
Closing	Be positive.	(3) _____ _____

Writing Your Message

Giving Details

When you tell customers about a change, be sure to say when the change will happen. Give as many details as possible.

Does not include details   We are moving our office.

Includes details   *As of March 1*, we are moving our *Malaysian office. . . . Please note the new address.*

Practice 2 Read the following openings for letters announcing a change in a company. Write which detail is missing.

1. We are moving our main office in May. Please note our new address.

   What day in May? _____

2. Two of our five European offices are closing on June 1.

   _____

3. Someone will call you on May 1 to discuss your new account.

   _____

4. On July 15, our Madrid office is moving.

   _____

5. Our telephone number is going to change to (768) 555-8979.

   _____

Time Markers and the Future Tense

Time markers are words or phrases that relate to time. When you use time markers to talk about something that is going to happen, use the future tense [*will* + simple present tense verb].

Your initial correspondence should mention a follow-up plan of action. This plan is usually written in the future and a time is specified.

> Your new account manager, Siling Wu, *will contact* you *shortly* to introduce herself and to answer any questions you might have.

Here are some examples of time markers.

shortly	in the near future
soon	within the month
tomorrow	after the holidays
in a few days	by the end of the week
within two weeks	at the beginning of next month

Practice 3

Rewrite the sentences using the future tense. Then circle the time markers.

1. The new sales director (be) in touch with you after the New Year holidays.

   The new sales director will be in touch with you

   after the New Year holidays.

2. I (call) you in a few weeks to discuss your concerns.

   _____

3. You (receive) an e-mail tomorrow from our new branch manager.

   _____

4. Customers (receive) an invitation to visit our new offices soon.

   _____

5. We (send) our new office directory so it will arrive before the end of the year.

   _____

That's Good Business!

Following up on a telephone call or letter gives you the chance to make a good impression. Follow-up communication helps to make relationships stronger and gives the customer another opportunity to do business with you.

Model E-Mail: Product Promotion

Look at the different elements of a product promotion announcement.

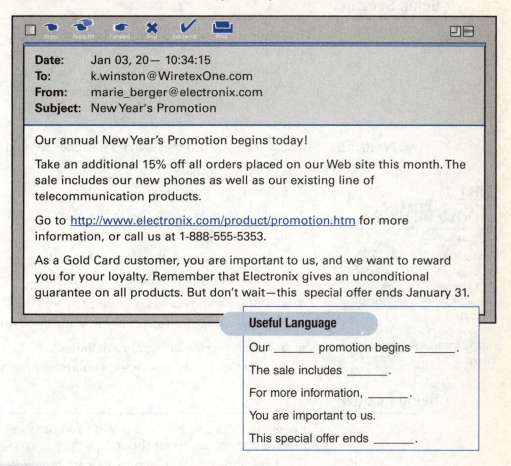

Date: Jan 03, 20— 10:34:15
To: k.winston@WiretexOne.com
From: marie_berger@electronix.com
Subject: New Year's Promotion

Our annual New Year's Promotion begins today!

Take an additional 15% off all orders placed on our Web site this month. The sale includes our new phones as well as our existing line of telecommunication products.

Go to http://www.electronix.com/product/promotion.htm for more information, or call us at 1-888-555-5353.

As a Gold Card customer, you are important to us, and we want to reward you for your loyalty. Remember that Electronix gives an unconditional guarantee on all products. But don't wait—this special offer ends January 31.

Useful Language

Our _____ promotion begins _____.

The sale includes _____.

For more information, _____.

You are important to us.

This special offer ends _____.

Composing Your Message

The body of a product promotion announcement generally has four parts.

Practice 4   Complete the chart using the Model E-Mail: Product Promotion.

Part	Content	Example
Opening	Tell why you are writing.	(1) _____ _____
Focus	Give details.	Take an additional 15% off all orders placed on our Web site this month. The sale includes our new phones as well as our existing line of telecommunication products.
Action	Tell how to get more information.	(2) _____ _____ _____
Closing	Be positive.	(3) _____ _____

Being Specific

The information in a customer relations letter should be as specific as possible.

Not specific	We'll give you a *discount*.
Specific	Take *an additional 15% off all orders placed on our Web site this month*.

Practice 5

Choose the sentence that is more personalized and specific.

1. **a.** Dear customer:
   b. Dear Ms. Romanov:

2. **a.** All orders taken in December earn 15% off.
   b. You could save thousands!

3. **a.** We will pay for shipping and handling for all orders over $2,000.
   b. Some customers will save on shipping.

4. **a.** Printer stands take an additional 10% off.
   b. Some computer furniture has additional savings.

5. **a.** Thank you for being our customer.
   b. As a Gold Card customer, you are our most valued client.

That's Good Business!

Look at the Model E-Mail on page 113. A customer relations letter should repeat the company's name and products' names several times.

Being Positive

A company's image is built up and promoted in its correspondence by using positive statements about the company.

Less positive	Electronix *stands behind its products*.
More positive	Remember that Electronix *gives an unconditional guarantee on all products*.

Practice 6

Choose the statement that is more positive.

1. **a.** At Grand Office, you can buy anything you need for your office.
   b. Grand Office is Asia's number one supplier of quality office furnishings.

2. **a.** We select each item we carry individually, to ensure quality and value for our customers.
   b. We buy from suppliers who sell many fine items.

3. **a.** Our goal is to have happy customers who return to us year after year for all of their office furnishing needs.
   b. Our goal is to keep you satisfied so that you will want to shop with us again.

4. **a.** We are looking for a few more customers.
   b. Our company and our success are built on customers like you.

That's Good Business!

It's easy to personalize letters using a computer program. A database can merge names and addresses with a form letter to create hundreds—or thousands—of personalized letters.

Look at the different elements of a letter announcing a product recall.

ELECTRONIX *INTERNATIONAL*

68, Jalan Sultan
50000 Kuala Lumpur
Malaysia

January 3, 20—

Ms. Cécile Marcil
Coolmail Now
32, rue de Meudon
92100 Boulogne-Billancourt
France

Subject: Product recall

Dear Ms. Marcil:

We are recalling the Photophone 642, which was shipped to you on December 5.

A chip in the product is defective and will be replaced.

We ask that you return all phones to us by January 31. Send them to our main distribution center. Please use overnight express, two-day air, or registered mail. Electronix will pay for all shipping and handling, plus give you a 10% discount on your next order. We will replace the defective chip and ship the Photophone back to you within 48 hours of receiving it.

We regret any inconvenience this recall may cause you. We look forward to continuing to provide you with the quality of electronic equipment that you expect. Please contact us if you have any questions.

Sincerely yours,

Marie Berger

Marie Berger
Division Manager, Asia and Europe

Useful Language

We are recalling _____.

_____ is defective and will be replaced.

We regret any inconvenience _____.

We look forward to continuing to provide you with _____.

Please contact us if you have any questions.

The body of a letter announcing a product recall generally has four parts.

Practice 7   Complete the chart using the Model Letter: Product Recall.

Part	Content	Example
Opening	Tell why you are writing.	(1) _____ _____
Focus	Give details.	(2) _____ _____
Action	Tell what will happen.	We ask that you return all phones to us by January 31. Send them to our main distribution center. Please use overnight express, two-day air, or registered mail. . . .
Closing	Be positive.	(3) _____ _____ _____ _____

Writing Your Message

Being Informative

A product recall is a serious matter. Be sure to include all of the important details regarding the recall. In particular, answer the questions *What? Why? When? Where?* and *How?*

What	We are recalling the Photophone 642.
Why	A chip in the product is defective and will be replaced.
When	We ask that you return all phones to us by January 31.
Where	Send them to our main distribution center.
How	Please use overnight express, two-day air, or registered mail.

Practice 8   Write which question these statements answer: *What, Why, When, Where,* or *How.*

1. _____ The internal antennae are defective.

2. _____ We are recalling wireless phones, model number 5342.

3. _____ Please return all phones by March 15.

4. _____ The shipment should be sent overnight express.

5. _____ Direct all inquiries to our customer service representatives.

Commas with Lists

Use a comma to separate three or more items in a list.

Please use *overnight express, two-day air,* or *registered mail.*
[1] [2] [3]

Some people do not use a comma before *or* and *and* between the last two items in a list. In this book, we use a comma. If you decide not to use this comma, make sure you are consistent within each piece of writing. If you use the comma in one sentence in a letter, then use it in other similar sentences.

Practice 9   Add commas to separate the items in each sentence.

1. Shipping handling taxes and return mailing fees will be covered.
2. Please return all pagers mobile phones and wireless devices whose serial numbers begin with *S.*
3. As always, we offer you quality goods competitive prices and professional service.
4. Our engineers have discovered defective screens keyboards and antennae.
5. We are recalling the following models: number 42S1B number 43D8C number 62S2B and number 58D8C.
6. Please call Mr. Lee Ms. Chin or Ms. Nieves if you have any questions.
7. We will be moving our office changing our phone number and updating our mailing list on January 2.

Complete the sentences in this letter. Use the words below.

attendees	complimentary	extend	location	meeting
business	considered	facilities	longtime	opportunity

125 Eden Street Bar Harbor, Maine 04609
Tel: 207-555-8983 Fax: 207-555-8985

Mr. L. Koogh
Events Planner
The Lamar Companies
870 Roundwood Drive
Scarborough, ME 04074

May 4, 20—

Dear Mr. Koogh:

The Vista Prix Conference Center is again open for (1) _____.
We are excited to announce our new (2) _____ in Bar
Harbor. We would like to (3) _____ an invitation to visit us
and meet our new director, Ms. Ingrid Bjorn. We hope all of our
(4) _____ customers will join us.

We invite you and a guest to our (5) _____ Sunday brunch.
This way, you can see first-hand why the Vista Prix is (6) _____
the best conference facility on the coast.

While you are here, visit Tech Avenue, where conference
(7) _____ can check e-mail or use computers for a minimal fee.
Thanks to our customers' highly valued comments, the Vista Prix knows
what it takes to be the best conference center, and is now able to offer
you the finest (8) _____.

We want the Vista Prix Conference Center to be the spot for your next
(9) _____. We look forward to the (10) _____ to
host you here at the Vista Prix.

Yours truly,

Malcolm Winer

Malcolm Winer
Customer Service Manager

Kay Wells sent a promotion letter about a new frequent flyer program. There are five places where Ms. Wells should be more specific and give more detail. On the lines below the letter, write the word or words that need more detail. Correct them so they will be more specific.

Isle Suns Airlines
Kansai International Airport
Building 2-banchi, Senshu-Kuko Kita
12, Izumisano-shi
Osaka 549 8501

January 19, 20—

Miss Lynn Sato
All Star Travel
1-1, 1-chome, Toyohira 4-Jo
Toyohira-ku
Sapporo 062 8521

(1)   Dear Customer:

You and your clients can now earn frequent flyer miles with Japanese
(2)   Airlines when you fly with Isle Suns Airlines. Travelers who fly this spring
(3)   will also get extra bonus miles.

(4)   In their recent partnership, these two airlines are combining efforts to
(5)   take you to Fiji, Guam, Hawaii, and Vanuatu. Soon, we'll even have
connecting flights to Papua New Guinea.

Travel agencies like All Star Travel can now book Isle travelers with just
one phone call, gain valuable mileage points, and enjoy the
convenience of easy connecting flights to these exciting destinations.

Japanese Airlines and Isle Suns appreciate your business, and we look
forward to serving all of your travel needs.

Sincerely yours,

Kay Wells

Kay Wells
Vice President, Customer Relations

1. _____

2. _____

3. _____

4. _____

5. _____

On a separate piece of paper, write a letter for one of these customer relations situations. Make up any specific information that is missing, such as the date the shipment was sent. Look in your local telephone book or on the Internet for names and addresses to use in your letter.

Jay,

Please send a note to all customers about our change of address. Ensure them that our commitment to prompt, effective service hasn't changed.

Sue

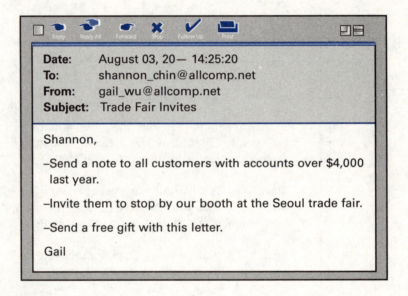

Date: August 03, 20— 14:25:20
To: shannon_chin@allcomp.net
From: gail_wu@allcomp.net
Subject: Trade Fair Invites

Shannon,

–Send a note to all customers with accounts over $4,000 last year.

–Invite them to stop by our booth at the Seoul trade fair.

–Send a free gift with this letter.

Gail

Words and Expressions to Know

Look at this list of words and expressions that were used in the unit. Their definitions are in the glossary at the end of the book.

change-of-address notice	preferred customer	take off
directory	pull	

Writing Personal Business Letters

Personal business letters are an important type of business correspondence. These letters and notes express thanks, congratulations, and condolences. They show concern and establish a social link between the writer and the recipient. For some occasions, such as birthdays and holidays, most business people do not write letters. They send greeting cards and add a short, personal note.

Before you write the letter, make sure you have all the right information. These letters are very important to the relationship between the writer and the recipient.

GETTING STARTED

1. Read the e-mails between an executive and her assistant. They discuss several personal business letters.
2. Complete the December calendar.

Date:	Dec 04, 20— 12:14:30
To:	jackien@securitynow.com
From:	lisar@securitynow.com
Subject:	Draft letters

Would you draft a thank-you letter to May Wing for referring us to Xenest? I want to send it out Monday.

Also, the father of Park Jeong-tae, CEO of PacMoon.com, passed away yesterday. Would you draft a condolence letter for me? I am at a loss for words. The letter needs to be sent today.

And, speaking of personal letters, did you order the New Year's greetings for our branches in Vietnam and China?

Date:	Dec 04, 20— 14:25:25
To:	lisar@securitynow.com
From:	jackien@securitynow.com
Subject:	Re: Draft letters

Lisa,

Sorry to hear about Jeong-tae's father. I'll draft a note this afternoon.

When you get a chance, would you drop by my office to sign Winsan's birthday card? He's turning 50 on the 16th.

Yesterday, I ordered the New Year's cards and also some general holiday greetings. That should take care of all of the religious holidays at the end of this month.

BTW, two days ago I sent the letter congratulating Hasan on his promotion.

Jackie

DECEMBER						
Sunday	**Monday**	**Tuesday**	**Wednesday**	**Thursday**	**Friday**	**Saturday**
	1	2	3	4	5	6
7	8	9	10	11	12	13
14	15	16	17	18 Hanukkah begins at sundown	19	20
21	22	23	24	25 Christmas Day	26 Boxing Day Kwanzaa begins	27
28	29 Ramadan begins	30	31 New Year's Eve			

Look at the different elements of a letter expressing thanks.

From the Desk of Lisa Rivelli

December 8, 20—

Dear May,

Thank you for referring us to Xenest Industries.

I met with Jae Yun last week in Beijing, and he is very interested in our security alarm systems. Not only does Xenest need security in its Beijing warehouse, but it also has storage centers in Fushun and in Harbin.

I hope to see you soon in Beijing so I can thank you personally for your introduction.

Again, thank you for putting me in touch with your contacts in Beijing.

Yours,
Lisa

Useful Language

Thank you for _____.

I hope to see you soon.

Again, thank you for _____.

The body of a letter expressing thanks generally has four parts.

Practice 1   Complete the chart using the Model Letter: Expressing Thanks.

Part	Content	Example
Opening	Tell why you are writing.	Thank you for referring us to Xenest Industries.
Focus	Give specific information.	(1) _____ _____ _____ _____ _____ _____
Action	Show appreciation.	(2) _____ _____ _____
Closing	Restate the main idea.	(3) _____ _____

Practice 2   Write *O* for Opening, *F* for Focus, *A* for Action, or *C* for Closing.

1. _____ Thanks for everything you did to make my first trip to Taiwan so enjoyable.

2. _____ I look forward to the opportunity to do you a similar favor.

3. _____ Again, I want to thank you for your kind and generous contribution.

4. _____ Your intern program gives students an opportunity to learn about the Internet.

5. _____ The entire staff join me in thanking you for sponsoring our weekend retreat.

6. _____ I must again say thanks for your support. It means a lot to me.

7. _____ The enclosed bonus check is a small token of my appreciation.

8. _____ The project was very difficult, but you and your team did a wonderful job.

That's Good Business!

Keep a list of major holidays in the countries where you have clients. When you mention the holiday or send an appropriate card, you show your clients that you care about them.

Look at the different elements of a letter expressing congratulations.

SecurityNow.com   605 Third Ave.   New York, NY   10158   212-555-8979 (phone)   212-555-8978 (fax)

December 2, 20—

Mr. Hasan Muhammad
Commercial Bank of Egypt
35 Sharia Qasr en-Nil
Cairo
Egypt

Dear Hasan,

Congratulations on your promotion to Vice President. All of us here who have known and worked with you over the years are pleased that you received the recognition you deserve.

When we first heard that Abbas Zaki resigned, we immediately thought of you for the position. Your many years of diligent service to Commercial Bank, and to the other banks where you've worked, show your commitment to quality banking in Egypt.

We look forward to continuing our working relationship with you and your bank.

Again, congratulations from all of us here at SecurityNow.com. Your promotion is richly deserved.

Yours,

Lisa Rivelli

Lisa Rivelli
President

Useful Language

Congratulations on _____.

All of us are pleased that _____.

We look forward to continuing our working relationship with you.

Again, congratulations _____.

The body of a letter expressing congratulations generally has four parts.

Practice 3   Complete the chart using the Model Letter: Expressing Congratulations.

Part	Content	Example
Opening	Tell why you are writing.	(1) _____ _____ _____
Focus	Personalize the information and be positive.	When we first heard that Abbas Zaki resigned, we immediately thought of you for the position. Your many years of diligent service to Commercial Bank, and to the other banks where you've worked, show your commitment to quality banking in Egypt.
Action	Refer to the future.	(2) _____ _____ _____ _____
Closing	Restate the main idea.	(3) _____ _____

Practice 4   Read these opening sentences for letters of congratulation. Then circle the letter of the closing sentence that best restates the main idea of the letter.

1. Congratulations on your retirement.
   a. When you first came to Acme, you worked in the mail room.
   b. Thank you for your many years of fine service to Banswell, Inc.

2. Let me congratulate you on the opening of your new offices in Tokyo.
   a. Your new branch in Japan shows that your hard work has paid off.
   b. The region should provide you with a lot of opportunities.

3. Congratulations on being the region's top sales rep this year.
   a. Your sales were over one million dollars this year.
   b. Given your hard work, you deserve this fine honor.

4. We congratulate you on winning the Customer Service Award.
   a. We want to thank you ourselves and tell you how pleased we are that your work has been recognized.
   b. We are just one of your new, and fully satisfied, customers.

5. All of us here at Winston and Bradley congratulate you on being made partner.
   a. When you were an intern here with us, we knew you would be a great lawyer.
   b. Being made partner is a privilege that you richly deserve.

Well SAID

The salutation and signature for a personal note should be more personalized and less businesslike than a standard business letter. In the salutation, address the person as if you were speaking to him or her directly.

Giving Praise

When you praise someone in a letter of congratulations, be specific. Avoid less specific words like *really*, *good*, *great*, *very*, and *a lot*.

Not specific	You did a really good job for Commercial Bank.
Specific	Your many years of diligent service to Commercial Bank, and to the other banks where you've worked, show your commitment to quality banking in Egypt.

Practice 5   Choose the sentence that is more specific.

1. **a.** You were a good teacher, and I learned a lot from you.
   b. Your detailed explanations helped me learn more effectively.

2. **a.** Your sales record looks really good, and your customers must be very happy.
   b. With the highest European sales for the year, you are clearly keeping your customers happy.

3. **a.** Your keen sense of timing and your careful research into market trends have made you one of Keeton's top marketers.
   b. You are really good at marketing and do great research, so we voted you as the best marketer at Keeton's.

4. **a.** It was obvious to me that your interpersonal skills and knowledge of the industry would not go overlooked.
   b. So somebody recognized your talents, did they?

5. **a.** Just as your offices are in other countries, your new Rome branch office will soon be a market leader.
   b. Rome is a good place to be so your new office might just be a big success.

6. **a.** It was a really good idea to promote you.
   b. The entire team at Bombay Exports will benefit from your promotion.

Well SAID

A personal note may be handwritten or typed, but it should always be signed by hand. A name stamp, computer-generated signature, or general signing, such as "From All of Us" may seem impersonal.

Look at the different elements of a letter expressing condolences.

December 4, 20—

Dear Jeong-tae,

I'm sorry to hear of your father's death.

I know that it is impossible to prepare for the loss of a parent.

I'm sure you have many good memories of your father, and when you think of him, you can take comfort in these memories.

Please accept my condolences. Please know that I'll also be keeping you in my thoughts.

Sincerely,

Lisa

Useful Language

I'm sorry to hear _____.

Please accept my condolences.

Please know that I'll also be keeping you in my thoughts.

The body of a letter expressing condolence generally has four parts.

Practice 6   Complete the chart using the Model Letter: Expressing Condolences.

Part	Content	Example
Opening	Tell why you are writing.	(1) _____ _____
Focus	Share your thoughts.	(2) _____ _____
Action	Offer a suggestion.	I'm sure you have many good memories of your father, and when you think of him, you can take comfort in these memories.
Closing	Restate the main idea.	(3) _____ _____ _____

Personal versus Professional

When sending a letter of condolence to a business associate, you can make the letter personal by using *I* or professional by using *we*. *We* includes your associates at work.

Personal   *I'm* sorry to hear of your father's death.

Professional   *We're* sorry to hear of your father's death.

Practice 7   Rewrite the sentences. Change the focus of the sentences from professional to personal.

1. The news of your father's death came as a surprise to us. You told us that he was sick, but his death must still be a shock.

   _____

   _____

2. Our thoughts and sympathies are with you as you mourn the loss of your father.

3. We hope that fond memories of him will help you through this difficult time.

   _____

4. My colleagues and I would like to extend our sympathy during this difficult time.

   _____

5. Please know that you have been in our thoughts, and accept our heartfelt condolences for your loss.

   _____

That's Good Business!

In a personal business letter, a writer who knows the recipient well may use an informal style. For example, you can use a first name followed by a comma in the salutation (*Dear Jeong-tae,*) and you can use contractions (*I'm*).

Prepositions

Be careful not to use the preposition *to* where you should use *at* or *of*.

Incorrect I'm sure you have many good memories of your father, and when you think *to* him, you can take comfort in these memories.

Correct I'm sure you have many good memories of your father, and when you think *of* him, you can take comfort in these memories.

Practice 8 Circle the prepositions in the sentences. If the preposition is wrong, correct it using *at* or *of*. Not all the prepositions are wrong.

1. I remember meeting your mother *at* (to) your firm's tenth anniversary party.

2. Although I knew your father had been ill for a long time, I was surprised to hear to his passing.

3. He was very proud to you, and he always wanted to talk about your success.

4. All of us will miss her sense to humor and her ability to get us all to work harder.

5. I will be to my son's wedding, so I can't come to the memorial service.

6. I will see you at the memorial service.

7. Everyone here at Sharma Industries was proud to your wife's success.

8. I often think to the time when your parents came to the office.

Well SAID

In general, a personal business note will be short if it addresses a sad situation, such as a death. However, personal notes are often longer when you are friends.

Write a personal business letter for one of the following situations.

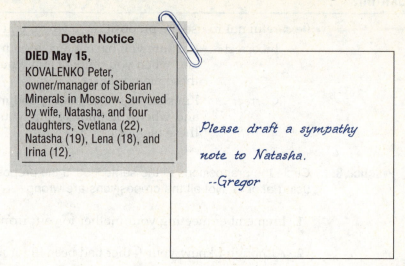

Death Notice

DIED May 15,
KOVALENKO Peter, owner/manager of Siberian Minerals in Moscow. Survived by wife, Natasha, and four daughters, Svetlana (22), Natasha (19), Lena (18), and Irina (12).

Please draft a sympathy note to Natasha.

--Gregor

Well SAID

Words are often abbreviated in short, informal messages especially between friends and co-workers.

you can become *u*

with can become *w/*

by the way can become *BTW*

congratulations can become *congrats*

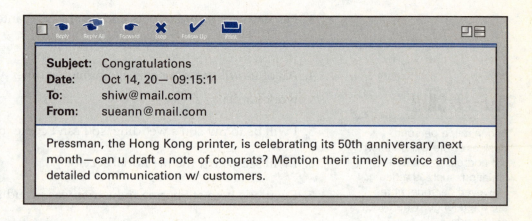

Subject: Congratulations
Date: Oct 14, 20— 09:15:11
To: shiw@mail.com
From: sueann@mail.com

Pressman, the Hong Kong printer, is celebrating its 50th anniversary next month—can u draft a note of congrats? Mention their timely service and detailed communication w/ customers.

Words and Expressions to Know

Look at this list of words and expressions that were used in the unit. Their definitions are in the glossary at the end of the book.

Boxing Day	Hanukkah	New Year's Eve	sponsor
Christmas	Kwanzaa	Ramadan	strengthen
commitment	mention	resignation	ties
drop by			

REFERENCE

Letter

Format The format of a piece of correspondence is the way it is organized and arranged. There are three formats for business correspondence: block, semi-block, and indented.

The format includes how the letter is typed and where the margins are. A margin is the blank space around a letter. There are four margins in a letter: top, bottom, left, and right. The format and the width of the margins will depend on your office stationery and office style.

Block This letter is written in block style. Everything begins at the left margin. This is called *flush left*.

Semi-Block This letter is written in semi-block style. Everything begins at the left margin, except for the date and the complimentary close and signature.

Indented This letter is written in indented style. Every paragraph is indented.

MNG Systems Inc.
Via Caballero, 7
20121 Milano
Italy
Tel: (02) 753264
Fax: (02) 753364

December 3, 20—

Ms. Rosa Tucci
General Television Service
Via Hoepli, 3
20121 Milano

Dear Ms. Tucci:

Thank you for your inquiry about our telephone answering machines and voice mail systems. I am enclosing brochures on our products.

A sales representative will be in your area next week. We will call you to schedule an appointment.

Again, thank you for your interest.

Sincerely yours,
Hazan Ozal
Hazan Ozal
Marketing Manager

cc: V. Alfonso, Sales Representative

WNM
Wilson New Media
P.O. Box 12456
Cheswick, Pennsylvania 15024
Phone (724) 555-8490 • Fax (724) 555-6652

August 16, 20—

Industrial Training Center
University of Exeter
Exeter EX1 2LU
United Kingdom

Dear Sir or Madam:

We read about your training programs in the *Training Gazette* of July 15. We train workers in the media industry in this country and are always looking for new materials.

We would appreciate receiving information on your Center and your training materials.

We look forward to hearing from you at your earliest convenience.

Sincerely yours,
Ralston Crawl
Ralston Crawl
Program Manager

Dodd Management Consulting Associates
3145 Theatre Road, North
RR4 Cobourg
Toronto, Ontario K9W 4J7
Canada

December 3, 20—

Shipping Manager
Complete Video
44 Stranger Street
Toronto, Ontario M4W 7L3

Dear Shipping Manager:

On November 2, we ordered six (6) flat screen color television sets. You sent us sixty (60).

We are returning fifty-four (54) of the sets to you today. We are requesting that you reimburse us for the cost of shipping these televisions back to you. Also, please correct the invoice.

Thank you for your attention to this matter.

Sincerely,
Tom Grayston
Tom Grayston
Purchasing Manager

Parts Look at the model letter on page 2. The letter is labeled with the letter parts below.

Return Address The return address contains:

Your street address: H Street

Your city, state and ZIP code: Washington, DC 20433

A comma separates the city from the state or country. A comma also separates the city or province from the country.

City, State: Berkeley, CA

City, Country: Madrid, Spain

City, Province, Country: Toronto, Ontario, Canada

Business letters usually have a printed letterhead. The letterhead has all of the company's information, including address, phone number, fax number, company Web site and personal e-mail address.

Date   The date of a letter is the date the letter is written. The date is below the return address. Always spell out the month in the date at the beginning of a business letter.

It is also better to spell out the month in dates in the body of the letter.   In correspondence between countries that use different styles, dates can be confusing when only numbers are used.

U.S. style	month/day/year
	January 12, 2005
	01/12/05
Non U.S. style	day/month/year
	12 January 2005
	12/01/05

Inside Address   The inside address contains the following addressee information:

Title, First Name, Last Name: Mr. Bill Rubin

Job Title: Vice President of Operations

Company Name: Garnet Educational Services

Street Address: 1525 Dexter Avenue, Suite 200

City, State ZIP Code: Seattle, Washington 98109

In the United States, the house or building number comes before the street name. In some countries, the number comes after the street name. In addition, when there is no state or province, include the country after the city.

Ms. Jan Hoisus
Manager, Public Relations Department
European Discs, Ltd.
Leliegracht, 46
1015 DH Amsterdam
Netherlands

Salutation   The salutation is the phrase, including the addressee's name, that is used at the beginning of a letter. Use a colon at the end of the name (*Dear Mr. Bhatia:*). There are three types of salutations:

Formal: Use a formal salutation if you do not know the person's name. Examples include: *Dear Sir or Madam* and *To Whom It May Concern.*

Standard: This is the most common type of salutation in business correspondence; use the person's title and last name. Examples include: *Dear Mr. Simar* and *Dear Dr. Patel.*

Informal: If you know the person well, use his or her first name. Examples include: *Dear Alexandra* and *Dear Jim.*

Body   The body of a letter tells why you are writing. There are generally four parts to the body of a letter.

Opening: Give your reason for writing.

Focus: Provide details about why you are writing.

Action: Tell what will happen next.

Closing: Thank the reader.

Complimentary Close   The complimentary close is the phrase you use after you end the body of the letter and before you sign your name. Like the salutation, there are three types of complimentary closes: formal, standard, and informal. The phrases *Sincerely, Sincerely yours,* and *Yours sincerely* can be used with any type of complimentary close. In addition, you can use *Yours very truly, Very truly yours, Very cordially yours,* and *Very sincerely yours* for formal complimentary closes. *Cordially* and *Yours truly* are appropriate for informal complimentary closes.

Signature/Typed Name   The writer's name and job title (or department) are typed at the bottom of the letter. He or she then signs the letter directly above the typed name.

Sometimes you will see two sets of initials at the bottom of a business letter. The first set is the writer's and is capitalized. The second set is the typist's and is lowercase. A slash separates the two sets of initials.

Writer/Typist   JP/rs

cc's   The letters *cc* stand for *carbon copy.* Carbon paper is a type of paper that was used to make copies before photocopiers and computer printers existed. Today, a "cc:" tells us who else received a copy of the letter. Note: *cc:* is not capitalized, and is always followed by a colon (:).

Folding a Letter

When a reader opens a business letter, the first thing he or she must see is the letterhead and date; the second is the body of the letter, and finally, the signature.

Fold a letter into three equal parts, like this:

1. Imagine where to divide the letter into three equal parts.

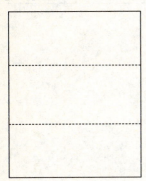

2. Fold the bottom of the letter to the top line.

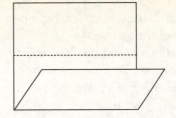

3. Fold the top third of the letter over.

Envelopes

Format   Most companies have envelopes with the companies' name and address pre-printed on them. The sender adds his or her name above or below the company address.

Parts

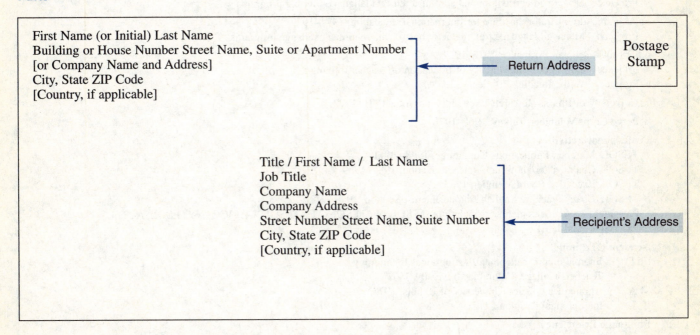

Résumé

Format
A résumé or curriculum vitae (c.v.) can be written in many different formats: outline, paragraph, or a combination of the two. The most common is the outline format. This format is the fastest to read, and it presents the information so it stands out easily.

Parts
A résumé should be short and clear. It should contain enough information to show that you are suited for the job and that the potential employer should invite you for an interview.

The following résumé is simple and contains the basic information: contact information, professional skills, professional experience, professional activities, academic training, and language proficiency.

Lin L. Lougheed
1775 Church St. NW
Washington, DC 20036-1301
(202) 332-5353
books@lougheed.com

Professional Skills

EFL/ESL material development	Multimedia instructional design
Multimedia material development	Skill training/cross-cultural awareness training

Professional Experience

1. President, Instructional Design International, Inc., 1983–present
   Projects: Consult with publishers, governmental agencies, and non-governmental agencies.
   Product: Develop and produce EFL/ESL textbooks, radio broadcasts, and online training programs.

2. English Teaching Officer, USIA, 1980–1983
   Projects: Consulted with U.S. Embassies and Missions overseas on the development of language training programs
   Product: Developed and produced teacher-training videotapes; wrote three language training texts and numerous training monographs

3. Fulbright Professor, Tunisia, 1979–1980
   Projects: Consulted with Ministry of Education on improvement of language teaching
   Product: Wrote English for science and technology text used by Tunisian universities in the science faculties

4. English Training Director, Educational Development Center, Boston, 1977–1979
   Projects: Developed curriculum and administered two language training programs

5. Program Administrator, Institute for International Education, 1974–1977
   Projects: Managed language training activities for international exchange programs

6. Fulbright Scholar, Sri Lanka, 1973–1974
   Projects: Consulted with Ministry of Education on teacher training
   Product: Wrote Reading Efficiency Text

7. University of Illinois Research Team, Teheran, Iran, 1971–1972

8. Peace Corps Volunteer, Turkey, 1968–1970

Professional Activities

TESOL, Member, Publications Committee, 1998–2000
TESOL, Chair, Materials Writers Interest Section, 1987–1989
TESOL, Executive Board Member, 1982–1985
TESOL, Chair, Teaching English Abroad Interest Section, 1979–1981
Presenter: Academic conferences including, TESOL, WATESOL, TEXTESOL, CALICO, NYTESOL, ACTFL, PRTESOL, and JALT

Academic Training

Ed.D.	International Development/Instructional Technology Teachers College, Columbia University, 1977
M.A.	Applied Linguistics, University of Illinois, 1973
B.A.	International Relations, UCLA, 1968

Language Proficiency

French: basic
Turkish: basic

Memos

Format A memo is generally correspondence written from one person in a company to another in the same company, or as an informal letter to someone outside the company. Block format is usually used.

Parts A memo generally has five parts:

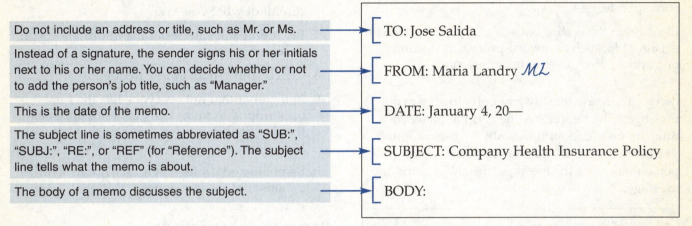

Do not include an address or title, such as Mr. or Ms.	TO: Jose Salida
Instead of a signature, the sender signs his or her initials next to his or her name. You can decide whether or not to add the person's job title, such as "Manager."	FROM: Maria Landry *ML*
This is the date of the memo.	DATE: January 4, 20—
The subject line is sometimes abbreviated as "SUB:", "SUBJ:", "RE:", or "REF" (for "Reference"). The subject line tells what the memo is about.	SUBJECT: Company Health Insurance Policy
The body of a memo discusses the subject.	BODY:

Faxes

Format A fax (short for *facsimile*) is a type of correspondence sent electronically through phone lines. A long fax is more expensive to send than a short one.

Most businesses have a separate telephone line for receiving and sending faxes. This is called a dedicated line. The telephone line is dedicated to the fax. When a fax has its own line, faxes can be received and sent 24 hours a day, seven days a week. In a small business or in homes, the fax may share a line with the telephone. It is less expensive to share one line, but it can cause delays.

Parts A fax transmission often has two parts.

Cover Sheet If a fax is more than one page, include a cover sheet. The cover sheet is the first page of the fax. This page may vary from company to company, but usually includes the following sections: addressee's name and title, sender's name and title, sender's fax and phone numbers, date, number of pages, subject/reference line, and message.

It is important to include how many pages are in the fax. The recipient needs to know if all the pages were sent. Examples include:

Pages: This + 2 (total 3 pages)

Pages: Cover + 4 (total 5 pages)

Pages: This only (total 1 page)

Pages: 5 (total 5 pages)

It is also important to include phone numbers on the cover sheet. If a page is missing or the fax is unclearly transmitted, you can call and ask the sender to fax it again.

Attachment An attachment is the material you are sending.

Addressee's Name	*Marta Cebula*
Addressee's Title	*Supply Manager*
Sender's Name	*Olga Kotwa*
Sender's Title	*Purchasing Supervisor*
Fax:	*620-03-85*
Phone:	*620-03-84*
Date:	*June 1, 20—*
Number of Pages:	*Cover + 1*

Subject Line:
June Purchase Order

Message:
See attached purchase order for our June shipment. Please call me at 620-04-12 when you receive this fax.

Electronic Mail (E-mail)

Format   Many companies send messages both internally and externally through their computers. These messages are called *electronic mail* or *e-mail.* E-mail is a fast and inexpensive way to communicate and a less formal method of correspondence.

In addition to sending messages, you can attach an existing file, such as a word-processed document or a spreadsheet, to an e-mail message.

Parts   There are usually five parts to an e-mail message. The sender's name and the date and time are provided automatically by the computer. The sender types in the e-mail address of the person receiving the message, the subject, and the message.

To:	mberry@helpinghands.com
From:	susanp@businesssolutions.com
Subject:	Business Opportunity
Date:	Mon, July 30, 20— 9:00 A.M.

Dear Mary,

Business Solutions is holding an open house on Friday. I think your group would benefit from the information and networking opportunities. I have attached the details of the meeting to this e-mail.

Hope to see you there.

Regards,
Susan

 Business Solutions
Open House

E-mail Guidelines

1. Don't send messages in all capital letters. Typing in all capital letters shows anger or impatience.

2. Try to respond to e-mails immediately. Let the sender know you've received the message. If you don't have time to respond completely, send a message saying when you will be able to respond.

3. Re-read your e-mails before you send them. Once they are sent, you can't get them back. Be careful of your tone. The recipient may not understand that you are saying something in a humorous way, for example.

4. Write a short and specific description of your message in the subject line.

5. If your e-mail program has a spell-check feature, use it.

6. Your message is not private. Other people can read it, either by mistake or on purpose. Your reader could send it to other people. Be careful of what you say.

7. Be careful and safe about the information you share over e-mail.

8. Check your e-mail in-box frequently.

9. Remember that not everyone has the same background as you. They may not understand that Dr. Pepper is a soft drink or that Kleenex is a tissue.

10. Be polite and professional. Try not to send e-mails that are very long.

Common Abbreviations

Abbreviation Punctuation

Use a period after a person's initial.

Thomas Lee Preston	T.L. Preston
Margaret Simpson Bates	Margaret S. Bates

Use a period after the following titles.
Mr.   Mrs.   Ms.   Dr.

Use a period after most abbreviations.

page, pages	p., pp.
Company	Co.
Corporation	Corp.
Incorporated	Inc.
Limited	Ltd.
number	no.
international	int'l.
ante meridiem	A.M.
post meridiem	P.M.
Manager	Mgr.
Department	Dept.
Secretary	Sec'y.

Some abbreviations do NOT use periods.

Eastern Standard Time	EST
As soon as possible	ASAP
Very important person	VIP
Close of business	COB
Personal computer	PC
Vice president	VP
Date of birth	DOB
Estimated time of arrival	ETA
To be determined	TBD
To be announced	TBA

Use a slash for some abbreviations.

05/16	May 16
c/o	care of
D/d	delivered
O/S	out of stock
n/a	not applicable
w/	with
w/out	without

U.S. Postal Abbreviations

States / Possessions

Alabama	AL
Alaska	AK
American Samoa	AS
Arizona	AZ
Arkansas	AR
California	CA
Colorado	CO
Connecticut	CT
Delaware	DE
District of Columbia	DC
Federal States of Micronesia	FM
Florida	FL
Georgia	GA
Guam	GU
Hawaii	HI
Idaho	ID
Illinois	IL
Indiana	IN
Iowa	IA
Kansas	KS
Kentucky	KY
Louisiana	LA
Maine	ME
Marshall Islands	MH
Maryland	MD
Massachusetts	MA
Michigan	MI
Minnesota	MN
Mississippi	MS
Missouri	MO
Montana	MT
Nebraska	NE
Nevada	NV
New Hampshire	NH
New Jersey	NJ
New Mexico	NM
New York	NY
North Carolina	NC
North Dakota	ND
Northern Mariana Is.	MP
Ohio	OH
Oklahoma	OK
Oregon	OR
Palau	PW
Pennsylvania	PA
Puerto Rico	PR
Rhode Island	RI
South Carolina	SC
South Dakota	SD
Tennessee	TN
Texas	TX
Trust Territories	TT
Utah	UT
Vermont	VT
Virginia	VA
Virgin Islands	VI
Washington	WA
West Virginia	WV
Wisconsin	WI
Wyoming	WY

Street Names

You may use street name abbreviations on envelopes, but you should spell out the names in letters.

Avenue	Ave.	Lane	Ln.
Boulevard	Blvd.	Parkway	Pkwy.
Center	Ctr.	Place	Pl.
Circle	Cir.	Road	Rd.
Court	Ct.	Route	Rte.
Drive	Dr.	Square	Sq.
Freeway	Fwy.	Street	St.
Highway	Hwy.	Terrace	Ter.

Months of the Year

January	Jan.	July	Jul.
February	Feb.	August	Aug.
March	Mar.	September	Sept.
April	Apr.	October	Oct.
May	May	November	Nov.
June	Jun.	December	Dec.

Days of the Week

Monday	Mon.	Friday	Fri.
Tuesday	Tues.	Saturday	Sat.
Wednesday	Wed.	Sunday	Sun.
Thursday	Thurs.		

Titles

Chief Executive Officer	CEO
Chief Financial Officer	CFO
Chief Information Officer	CIO
Assistant Vice President	AVP

Monetary Units

Country	Monetary Unit	Symbol
Australia	dollar	A$
Brazil	real	R
Canada	dollar	Can$
Costa Rica	colon	C
Czech Republic	korona	K
Egypt	Egyptian pound	£E
Hong Kong	dollar	HK$
India	Indian rupee	Re
Japan	yen	¥
Kenya	Kenya shilling	KSh
Mexico	peso	Mex$
Morocco	Dirham	DH
New Zealand	dollar	NZ$
Poland	zloty	Zl
Russia	ruble	Rb
Singapore	dollar	S$
South Africa	rand	R
South Korea	won	W
Switzerland	franc	SFr
Taiwan	dollar	NT$
United Kingdom	pound sterling	£
United States	dollar	US$

The following countries use the euro
(as of June 2002).

Country		Monetary Unit	Symbol
Austria	Ireland	euro	€
Belgium	Italy		
Finland	Luxembourg		
France	the Netherlands		
Germany	Portugal		
Greece	Spain		

Internet Domain Names

Here are some Internet domain names and the types of institutions they are usually associated with. New domain names are regularly added as more individuals and institutions use the Internet.

.biz   business
.co   company (outside the United States)
.com   company
.edu   educational institution
.gov   government (U.S.)
.info   information service
.int   international organization
.mil   military (U.S.)
.name individual
.net   network
.org   organization

Reading Aloud

Slash (/)

1. A slash (/) means "for [each]" or "per" when a number comes before it. For example, $29.95/carton means the price is $29.95 for each carton.

$22.45/dozen	$22.45 for each dozen _or_ $22.45 per dozen
$13.66/gross	$13.66 for a gross _or_ $13.66 per gross
$1.95/box	$1.95 for each box _or_ $1.96 per gross

Say "for" when a number follows the slash.

$9.88/2	$9.88 for two

2. A slash (/) means "and" when it separates two nouns.

Shipping/Handling = Shipping and Handling

Shipping/Handling is the cost to prepare, pack, and send an order. It is usually a percentage of the total cost of the order.

ASAP

ASAP means "as soon as possible."

Say only the letters "A-S-A-P" or "as soon as possible."

Ext.

Ext. means telephone extension number

Say "extension." (_Her number is 914.555.8000, extension 8093._)

X and =

X means by _or_ times   = means equals

8 1/2" x 11" = 8 1/2 inches wide by 11 inches tall

10 x 2 = 20 = ten times two equals 20

GLOSSARY

Following each word is the unit number where the word first appears.

Accessory, 7 (n) something you add to a machine, tool, car, etc. to make it more useful: *I put the writing accessories, like the pens and paper, in the desk.*

Accommodate, 3 (v) to have enough space for a particular number of people or things: *The table in our conference room can accommodate eighteen people.*

Account, 9 (n) a list of fiscal transactions: *We will credit your account for the damaged goods.*

Acknowledge, 2 (v) to accept or admit that something is true or that a situation exists: *The shipping department manager acknowledges that they're not working efficiently.*

Adjustment letter, 10 (n) a letter settling a debt or claim: *Send an adjustment letter to the client whose shipment was damaged. Tell him we'll credit his company's account.*

Apology, 10 (n) something that you say or write to say that you are sorry: *I'm truly sorry for getting angry during our meeting. Please accept my apology.*

Applicant, 2 (n) somebody who has formally asked for a job, especially by writing a letter: *I've read all these résumés. Now let's schedule an interview for each applicant.*

Apply [something] against, 5 (v) to charge somebody some money by taking it out of his or her wages, bank account, etc.: *The boss is applying the cost of replacing the cell phone you lost against your next paycheck.*

Attach, 1 (v) to make something stick to or be connected with something else: *Please attach a list of references to your résumé.*

Attention, 10 (n) the special care you give to someone or something: *My secretary is an excellent employee because of the attention that he gives to detail.*

Authorization, 12 (n) official permission to do something: *Did the Board of Directors give you authorization to sign that agreement?*

Back order, 6 (v) to put an item that a customer ordered on a list because the company has no more of it. The company sends it out later when they get more: *The item is out of stock, so we will back order it for you.*

Balance, 5 (n) the amount of something that remains after some has been used, paid, or spent: *You owed $100; you paid $75. There is a balance of $25 to pay.*

Behind schedule, 6 (prepositional phrase) not as successful or advanced as planned: *The contract says we will lose 5% of our money for every week we're behind schedule.*

Bill, 9 (v) to send a list of how much money someone owes: *Clients are billed once a month.*

Boxing Day, 15 (n) the first weekday after Christmas observed as a legal holiday in Great Britain, Australia, New Zealand, and Canada: *My family always donates to the poor on Boxing Day.*

Branch, 13 (n) one part of something larger such as an organization or a family: *Our bank has branches in London, Paris, and Singapore.*

Brochure, 7 (n) a thin book that gives information or advertises something: *The new tourist attraction delivered brochures to all the major hotels.*

Cancel, 9 (v) to say or decide that something you have planned will not happen: *If more guests cancel their reservations, this hotel will be in trouble.*

Candidate, 1 (n) someone who applies for a job or is trying to be elected to a political position: *Williams is a good candidate for the financial officer position.*

Carry, 7 (v) to have something that is available for people to use or buy: *Our store used to carry that brand of VCR, but we don't anymore.*

Change-of-address notice, 14 (n) a written or printed statement that informs people that somebody has moved: *You can get packets of change-of-address notices from your local post office.*

Chip set, 6 (n) a group of computer chips that belong or are used together: *This chip set is no good. It has one piece missing.*

Christmas, 15 (n) December 25, the day when Christians celebrate the birth of Jesus Christ: *Anna went to the mall to buy Christmas gifts.*

Claim letter, 9 (n) a letter officially asking for money that you have a right to receive: *Send a claim letter to our insurance company for the cargo that was ruined in the flood.*

Clarification, 8 (n) making something easier to understand by explaining it in more detail: *We don't understand two things in this contract. We would like clarification on Sections 5 and 8.*

Colleague, 1 (n) someone you work with: *Ms. Ames and I work in the same law firm. We've been colleagues for six years.*

Collection agency, 11 (n) a company that finds people who owe money to other businesses and forces them to pay it: *We have asked for payment three times, but you have sent us nothing. If we don't receive payment within two weeks, we will give this matter to a collection agency.*

Commitment, 15 (n) a promise to do something or behave in a particular way: *We provide great service and guarantee our products. This is our commitment to our customers.*

Complimentary, 10 (adj) given free to people: *All guests receive a complimentary breakfast.*

Concise, 6 (adj) short and clear, without using too many words: *I like the manager because his instructions and explanations are always concise.*

Confirm, 3 (v) to say or prove that something is definitely true: *This letter will confirm the details of our telephone conversation.*

Confirmation, 3 (n) a statement or letter that says that something is definitely true: *We haven't received confirmation that the main office has approved the merger.*

Confusion, 12 (n) a state of not understanding what is happening or what something means: *There is confusion over Sections 5 and 8 of the contract. That is why we need clarification.*

Contact, 13 (n) someone you know who may be able to help you or give you advice: *Don't worry about opening your new business in Detroit. I have many contacts in that city.*

Continuity, 8 (n) the state of continuing over a long period of time without changing: *This company wants continuity in its sales policies. We've been doing business the same way for decades.*

Courier, 9 (n) someone who delivers messages: *We use a courier to deliver important documents between our New York and London offices.*

Credit, 10 (n) an arrangement with a bank or store that allows you to buy something and pay for it later: *We have credit with all the companies that supply raw materials to our factories.*

Credit, 9 (v) to add money to an account: *We are crediting your account for the defective parts you purchased last month.*

Customer service, 10 (n) the department within a company that helps customers and tries to keep them satisfied: *If you have any questions about your new cell phone, call our Customer Service Department and they'll be happy to help you.*

Directory, 14 (n) a book or list of names, facts, events, etc., arranged in alphabetical order: *Here's the directory of all of our stores. Use it to prepare the mailing about our annual meeting.*

Distributor, 7 (n) a company or person that supplies goods to stores or other companies: *I used to work for a large distributor of auto parts.*

Drop by, 15 (v) to visit informally and unexpectedly: *The next time I'm in town, I'll drop by to discuss your inventory concerns.*

Employee announcement, 13 (n) an official public statement made by workers in a company: *We have a bulletin board in the lunchroom where we post employee announcements about personal matters like births and weddings.*

Employee relations, 13 (n) the way employees behave toward one another: *Our Human Resources Department deals with any problems concerning employee relations.*

Equivalent, 2 (n) something that has the same value or size as something else: *You must have a high school degree or its equivalent, for example, a passing score on a test like the GED.*

Estimate, 4 (n) a statement of how much it will probably cost to build or repair something: *We aren't sure how much it will cost, so we've given the client an estimate.*

Expect, 4 (v) to think that something will happen: *I'm expecting all company officers to be at the meeting. I hope everyone will come.*

Extend, 13 (v) to offer someone help, thanks, sympathy, etc.: *Let's extend a warm welcome to Ms. Dodson, our new vice president for marketing!*

Fax, 3 (v) to send a document in electronic form down a telephone line from one special machine to another: *You can fax me the letters of credit this afternoon. I'll be in my office until 4.*

Firm, 11 (n) a business or small company: *Mr. Kelly founded this accounting firm in 1975.*

Flyer, 8 (n) a sheet of paper advertising something: *Small businesses like to place flyers under the windshields of cars to advertise cheaply.*

Follow through, 13 (v) to do what needs to be done to complete something or make it successful: *The CEO promised to improve workers' benefits, but he never followed through.*

Follow-up, 1 (n): *The Equal Opportunity Commission is doing a follow-up of the company's unusual hiring practices by re-interviewing various employees.*

Follow up, 1 (v) to find out more or do more about something: *The Equal Opportunity Commission investigated the company's unusual hiring practices. Now they're following up by re-interviewing various employees.*

Forward, 8 (v) to send a message or give information to the person it was intended for: *I will forward the new sales figures to Bob.*

Fulfill, 8 (v) to make something become true or cause something to happen: *If the owner doesn't receive the loan, he'll never fulfill his dream of doubling the size of the company.*

Good for, 10 (expression) representing equal value: *This coupon is good for $10 off my next purchase.*

Goods, 5 (n) things that are produced in order to be sold: *What kinds of goods does that store sell?*

Hanukkah, 15 (n) an eight-day Jewish holiday in December: *My family is visiting us the first night of Hanukkah.*

Headquarters, 11 (n) the office that is the center of a large organization: *The bank has branches all over the world, but its headquarters are in Berlin.*

In stock, 5 (prepositional phrase) available to buy (as with merchandise in a store): *This supermarket always has fresh produce in stock.*

In touch, 8 (expression) communicating with someone by telephone, letter, e-mail, etc.: *All stores are in touch with our main office on a daily basis.*

Inconvenience, 6 (n) something that causes you problems or difficulties, or the state of having problems or difficulties: *I'm sorry your item has been back ordered; we apologize for any inconvenience.*

Indicate, 4 (v) to show that something exists or is likely to be true: *Consumers are spending more, which indicates they have confidence in the economy.*

Initial, 8 (adj) happening at the beginning; first: *The initial customer response to our latest TV commercial has been quite good.*

Inquiry, 8 (n) the act of asking questions in order to get information about something: *The government plans to hold an inquiry into irregularities in our tax records.*

Installment, 12 (n) one of a series of regular payments that you make until you have paid all the money you owe: *The boss is paying back the business loan he got from the bank in quarterly installments.*

Invoice, 9 (n) a list that shows how much you owe for goods, work, etc.: *When the Shipping Department prepares merchandise to send to our customers, they include an invoice in each box.*

Keep [something] on file, 2 (verb phrase) to save information in a file so that it can be used later: *Our Human Resources Department keeps applications from job seekers on file for one year.*

Kwanzaa, 15 (n) a seven-day holiday celebrated December 26-January 1 by Africans and African-Americans around the world: *The community center is having a Kwanzaa festival.*

Letter of introduction, 13 (n) a letter from someone you trust that introduces somebody to you who you don't know: *When the comptroller applied for that position, he gave the Human Resource Department a letter of introduction from one of our CEO's old business associates.*

Letter of reference, 13 (n) a letter containing information about you that is written by someone whom knows you well, usually to a new employer: *You must give the company two letters of reference from business associates and one from a personal associate.*

Look over, 3 (v) to examine someone or something quickly: *Our manager looks over job applicants' credentials and letters of reference before scheduling interviews.*

Make an adjustment, 9 (verb phrase) to make a small change to something: *Since your order was incomplete, we have made an adjustment to your invoice.*

Make the most of, 10 (expression) to get the most advantage that is possible from a situation: *Offices are quite small here, so you'll have to make the most of the space you have.*

Make up, 5 (verb phrase) to prepare or arrange something: *Please make up a new schedule for next week's meetings.*

Meet the requirement, 2 (verb phrase) to have or do enough of what is needed: *The head of Human Resources thinks that last candidate should get the job. She meets all the requirements for the position.*

Mention, 15 (v) to say or write about something in a few words: *Our company was mentioned in the article about the ten best companies in this city.*

Negotiable, 4 (adj) can be changed through discussion (like prices or agreements): *Contracts for top corporate positions are always negotiable when they are ready for renewal.*

New Year's Eve, 15 (n) the night before the first day of the calendar year: *Marco is having a big New Year's Eve party.*

Notice, 11 (n) a written or printed statement that gives information or a warning to people: *We got a notice in the mail that our check had not been received.*

On hand, 5 (expression) close and ready to be used when needed: *The secretary always has extra ink cartridges on hand for her computer printer.*

On the market, 7 (expression) available for someone to buy: *Our company's latest vacuum cleaner will on the market by the end of the summer.*

Opening, 1 (n) a job or position that is available: *Since Ms. James quit, I have an opening for a secretary.*

Option, 7 (n) a choice you can make in a particular situation: *We offer various payment options: cash, personal check, money order, or credit card.*

Order form, 8 (n) a sheet of paper that is used to list a request for goods from a company: *Our company's catalog contains a simple order form that customers can fill out and send in.*

Out of stock, 6 (prepositional phrase) not available to buy (as with merchandise in a store): *I'm sorry, but the brand of toothpaste you want is out of stock. Would you like another brand?*

Owe, 12 (v) to have to pay someone because he or she has allowed you to borrow money: *The owner of the company owes the bank $30,000 on the loan he got to expand the business.*

Paid in full, 12 (expression) paid for completely; not owing any more money: *This is the last installment you have to pay. I'm writing "paid in full" on your receipt.*

Partial, 11 (adj) not complete: *This is a partial list of our inventory. I'll have the rest for you by tomorrow.*

Pay upon receipt, 5 (verb phrase) to pay for something when you receive it: *The vendor says we don't need to pay them yet; we can pay upon receipt of the goods.*

Photocopy, 12 (n) a copy of a document made by a photocopier: *We lost the original letter, but we have a photocopy to refer to.*

Point out, 9 (v) to tell someone something that he or she does not already know or has not yet noticed: *The boss pointed out to Murphy that his sales are down.*

Post, 1 (v) to put a public notice about something on a wall or bulletin board: *You can post announcements, like job openings, on the Internet, either on a Web page or in a chat room.*

Preferred customer, 14 (n) a customer that a company likes because he or she pays for goods without problems: *Because you're a preferred customer, we'd like to offer you a special discount on this new line of dresses.*

Price list, 8 (n) a list of prices for goods or services that are offered: *Here's a price list of all the services our spa offers to our clients.*

Process, 5 (v) to deal with information in an official way: *We will process your order as soon as it is received.*

Proficient, 1 (adj) able to do something with a high level of skill: *One reason that Schwartz does so well in our international sales department is that she's proficient in French, German, and Arabic.*

Projected, 3 (adj) calculated or planned for what will happen in the future: *The value of our stock has gone up because of the projected profits for the next fiscal year.*

Pull, 14 (v) retrieve from database: *During the official government inquiry, investigators pulled the files on all current employees.*

Ramadan, 15 (n) the ninth month of the Islamic year observed as sacred, with fasting daily from dawn to sunset: *Ahmad always fasts during Ramadan.*

Rate, 3 (n) a charge or payment set according to a standard scale: *The hotel room rates started at $60 for a single room and went to $300 for a suite.*

Receive, 9 (v) to be given something: *The warehouse manager says that the invoice was missing from the last shipment he received.*

Reference line, 6 (n) a short statement near the top of a memorandum (memo) that gives the reason for writing: *At the beginning of the reference line in a memorandum, it's customary to use the abbreviation* Re: *which stands for "regarding."*

Refund, 10 (n) an amount of money that is given back to you if you are not satisfied with the goods or services you have paid for: *When I returned that defective fax machine to the store, I was given a full refund.*

Regret, 6 (v) to be sorry and sad about a situation: *We regret that the computer was damaged in shipping; we will replace it.*

Rejection, 2 (n) the act of not accepting someone for a job, school, etc., or not accepting something: *Because of his age, our plant manager received four rejections before he got this job.*

Reliable, 13 (adj) able to be trusted; dependable: *The boss only wants reliable workers who won't come in late.*

Reminder, 11 (n) something that makes you notice or remember something else: *My secretary always writes himself little notes as reminders so he won't forget to do things.*

Remit, 11 (v) to send a payment by mail: *Please remit payment to P.O. Box 144, Bellows Falls, VT 05101*

Reputation, 12 (n) the opinion that people have of someone or something because of what has happened in the past: *Other car dealers are always trying to attract Bob to work for them because of his reputation as one of the best salespeople.*

Requirement, 1 (n) a quality or skill that is needed or asked for in a particular situation: *The foreman lacks one requirement to become plant supervisor. He never completed high school.*

Reschedule, 2 (v) to change the plan for something to happen at a particular time: *I have to reschedule your appointment for an interview because I must go out of town for a week.*

Reserve, 3 (v) to arrange for a place in a hotel, on a plane, etc. to be kept for you to use: *I need a hotel room when I attend the conference. Please call the hotel and reserve a suite for me.*

Resignation, 15 (n) a written statement saying you are leaving your job or position officially because you want to: *Because funds had been misplaced or lost, the comptroller gave her resignation to the CEO's secretary.*

Restate, 4 (v) to say something again in a different way so that it is clearer or more strongly expressed: *The CEO restated her opinion when it became clear to her that the Board members did not understand her position.*

Return, 8 (v) to do something similar: *If you call me and leave a message, I will return your call as soon as possible.*

Review, 2 (v) to examine, consider, and judge a situation, process, or person carefully: *We are reviewing the list of candidates to see who should come in for an interview.*

Satisfaction, 10 (n) a feeling of happiness or pleasure because you have achieved something or gotten what you wanted: *Our company's reputation is based on one thing: constant customer satisfaction.*

Search, 2 (n) an attempt to find someone or something that is difficult to find: *The Board of Directors is planning to do a search for a new marketing director.*

See, 3 (v) to find out information or a fact: *Before we decide to hire more workers, let's see if business keeps increasing.*

Set apart, 7 (v) to make someone or something different from other similar people or things: *What sets our appliance store apart from others is the number of legitimate sales we have per year.*

Shipped, 7 (v) to send or deliver (such as merchandise): *We ship ceramic giftware from our factory to our stores once a month.*

Shipping and handling, 9 (n) the price charged for delivering goods: *Please add 12% to the total for your order to pay for shipping and handling.*

Source, 7 (n) the thing, place, person, etc. that you obtain something from: *The source of the rubber we use is a large plantation in Brazil.*

Sponsor, 15 (v) to give someone money for a worthy cause: *We need someone to pay for our expenses; someone who will sponsor our development costs.*

Strengthen, 15 (v) to become stronger or more valuable, or to make something stronger or more valuable: *The company is strengthening its financial stability by closing down its unprofitable stores.*

Subject line, 6 (n) a brief statement or phrase explaining the reason for sending an e-mail, etc.: *The subject line of an e-mail is the same as a reference line in a memorandum.*

Substitute, 6 (v) to use something new or different instead of something else: *The model X-12 is unavailable. May we substitute model X-13, which is very similar?*

Take off, 14 (v) to reduce by a certain amount: *Our company takes 20% off all products purchased by students preparing to enter our profession.*

Ties, 15 (n) a relationship between two people, groups, or countries: *Our importing company has close ties with factories in Spain, Portugal, and Italy.*

Under pressure, 13 (adv.) affected by a particular influence, condition, or situation: *It was 10 a.m. and we had to finish the project by noon, but we always perform well under pressure.*

Under separate cover, 8 (prepositional phrase) sent separately from the message you are reading: *Please be advised that the documents you've requested are being sent under separate cover.*

Unfortunate, 12 (adj) happening because of bad luck: *We're sorry that the goods arrived damaged; we regret this unfortunate incident.*

Unspecified, 13 (adj) not clearly or definitely stated: *The deadline for that project was unspecified.*

Upgrade, 6 (v) to improve something, or to exchange something for something better: *Your computer now uses the OS 7.5 operating system, but you can upgrade it to OS 8.0.*

Vacancy, 1 (n) a job that is available for someone to start doing: *The Marketing Department advises me that they now have a vacancy since Ms. Collins retired.*

Waive, 5 (v) to state officially that a right or rule can be ignored: *She waived her right to ask for an extension on the schedule.*

ANSWER KEY

TEST YOURSELF, page v

1. Date; Inside Address; Salutation; Body; Complimentary Close; Signature; Name; Job Title

2. This letter is in block style.

3. 1.August **2.** 15, (comma) **3.** Mr. **4.** M. **5.** Soup **6.** Angeles **7.** Dear **8.** Mr. **9.** Ramirez: (colon) **10.** Your; **11.** morning. (period) **12.** Add "Please" before "tell" **13.** airport (period instead of question mark) **14.** yours, (comma) **15.** Bill

---

UNIT 1, page 1

Getting Started, page 1

1.Web site ad and Newspaper ad **2.** Newspaper ad **3.** Web site ad and Newspaper ad **4.** Web site ad **5.** Newspaper ad **Your skills:** Answers will vary.

Practice 1, page 3

1. c. Note: **a** is also appropriate in style and content; **b** may be true, but the statement is too desperate to use in a letter applying for a job.

2. a. Note: **c** is also appropriate in style and content; **b** may be true, but the statement "never worked before" would not impress a reader. Try, "I'm a recent graduate of Barton High School where I was known for learning new skills very quickly."

3. b. Note: **a** is also appropriate in style and content; **c** may be true, but the expression "if you need me" does not carry the right tone. Try, "Please feel free to call me at home (212) 555-1234 to schedule an interview."

4. c. Note: **b** is also appropriate in style and content; **a** is too flippant.

Practice 2, page 4

2. Dear Recruiter: **3.** Dear Ms. Bowles: **4.** Dear Chee Yu:

Practice 3, page 4

1. for; in **2.** for; on **3.** On; about; for **4.** about

Practice 4, page 5 *Answers will vary, depending on individual skills.*

2. I have a college degree and am familiar with word processing programs.

3. I have excellent communication skills.

4. I have strong organizational skills.

5. I have graduated from high school and worked in an office for three years.

Practice 5, page 5

1. G **2.** S **3.** G **4.** S **5.** S

Practice 6, page 5

2. I look forward to talking to you next week. **3.** I look forward to meeting with you. **4.** I look forward to discussing with you my interest in A-Way. **5.** I look forward to contributing to your team.

Letter Practice 1, page 6

1. Resource **2.** applying **3.** part-time **4.** enclosed **5.** interview **6.** forward **7.** position **8.** Sincerely

Letter Practice 2, page 7

2. Recruiter: (colon) **3.** to **4.** on **5.** for **6.** secretaries **7.** software. (period) **8.** application **9.** hearing **10.** Sincerely

Letter Practice 3, page 8

Letters will vary but must follow the model letter format.

UNIT 2, page 9

Getting Started, page 9

1. I **2.** R **3.** R **4.** R **5.** I **6.** R **7.** R **8.** I **9.** I **10.** R **You:** *Answers will vary.*

Practice 1, page 12

1. b. I c. I d. A, I, R **2.** a. A b. R c. A d. I **3.** a. I b. A, I, R c. R d. A, I, R

Practice 2, page 13

1. a and b are appropriate in style and content; c is OK, but is unlikely. Usually the writer would not identify who opened an application.

2. a and c are appropriate in style and content; b uses the word "trying," which is not the word a writer would use in this instance.

3. a and b are appropriate in style and content; c is not appropriate. "Want" should be "would like" and "sometime" should be replaced with a phrase that suggests convenience for the reader, such as "at a time convenient for you."

4. a and b are appropriate in style and content; c is not formal enough. "Hi!" would not be used in a business letter. Similarly the expression "It's great" is too informal for this type of letter.

5. b and c are appropriate in style and content; a contains the expressions "check out" and "really happy." Both are too informal.

Practice 3, page 14

2. A; a **3.** I; b **4.** A; b **5.** I; a **6.** R; c **7.** I; c **8.** A; a **9.** R; b **10.** R, b **11.** I, a **12.** A, c

Practice 4, page 15 *Answers may vary.*

2. Thank you for your interest in the position available with NetLives.

3. I wish you the all best with your job search.

4. I look forward to meeting you on Thursday.

5. I look forward to discussing the position with you.

6. We will keep your résumé on file should a position meeting your qualifications become available.

7. Thank you for your interest in IronGate.com.

Letter Practice 1, page 16

1. received **2.** response **3.** advertisement **4.** applicant **5.** résumé **6.** openings **7.** wish **8.** search

Letter Practice 2, page 17

1.delete Sandy **2.** Hill: (colon) **3.** for **4.** assistant **5.** now **6.** notify **7.** you **8.** Sincerely, (comma) **9.** Title should be on line below name **10.** Maki Ishii should be before her title

Letter Practice 3, page 18

Letters will vary but must follow the model letter format.

UNIT 3, page 19

Getting Started, page 19

1. Curt Marks **2.** cmarks@cellfirst.com **3.** March 15 **4.** March 16 **5.** 80 **6.** 1 **7.** 3 **8.** 5 **9.** 80 **10.** 1 **11.** 1 **12.** 0 **13.** 0 **14.** 1 **15.** None **16.** Lunch: March 16; 80 **17.** None **18.** Coffee breaks; March 15 and March 16; 80

Practice 1, page 21

1. C **2.** F **3.** A **4.** O **5.** O **6.** A **7.** C **8.** F **9.** F **10.** O **11.** C **12.** A **13.** A **14.** C **15.** F **16.** O

Practice 2, page 22

1. for **2.** at **3.** on *or* by **4.** in **5.** of **6.** on

Practice 3, page 22

1. a **2.** b **3.** a **4.** a **5.** a **6.** b **7.** b **8.** a

Practice 4, page 23 *Answers will vary.*

2. Would/could you please send me the cost projections by June 1?

3. Would/could you please be able to provide lunch on Saturday?

4. Would/could you please have three additional rooms available for break-out meetings on Monday?

5. Would/could you please provide the price per person for the coffee breaks by tomorrow?
6. Would/could you please put audiovisual equipment in the three smaller break-out rooms Friday?
7. Would/could you please e-mail me the cost per person by 5 o'clock today?
8. Would/could you please get back to me on the dates of the training seminar by May 15?
9. Would/could you please add two more speakers in the large room today?
10. Would/could you please tell me the total number of attendees by next Thursday?

Practice 5, page 23
2. I look forward to receiving your fax before the end of the day.
3. I look forward to receiving your letter within the next two weeks.
4. I look forward to receiving a phone call at your earliest convenience.
5. I look forward to meeting you on March 7th.

Letter Practice 1, page 24
1. conversation 2. confirm 3. take place 4. approximately 5. rooms
6. available 7. possible 8. forward

Letter Practice 2, page 25
1. Glass: (colon) 2. will 3. receive
4. There 5. we 6. schedule 7. to
8. send to my attention 9. forward
10. Sincerely, (comma)

Letter Practice 3, page 26
Letters will vary but must follow the model letter format.

UNIT 4, page 27

Getting Started, page 27
1. 2/4 2. Client is bringing own computer 3. 2/4 4. A buffet lunch is OK.

Practice 1, page 29
1. a and c are appropriate in style and content; b is too forward, almost impolite.
2. a and b are appropriate in style and content; c is too general. If the writer needs information, try, "Please fax me your needs so I can address them fully."
3. a and c are appropriate in style and content; b may be true, but it contains general information, rather than the Action.
4. a and c are appropriate in style and content; b is appropriate for the Action.

Practice 2, page 29
2. You refers to Curt Marks; we refers to Turner and Arrowhead.
3. Us refers to Turner and Arrowhead.
4. You refers to Curt Marks; I refers to Jan Turner.

5. I refers to Turner; Your refers to Marks and CellFirst.

Practice 3, page 30
2. e 3. a 4. d 5. c

Practice 4, page 31 *Answers will vary.*
2. Please let us know whether you want rectangular or round tables.
3. We can provide either NSTC or PAL VCR format.
4. Please tell us if you want coffee breaks in the mornings, afternoons, or both.
5. We need to know whether you would like the chairs to be placed theater style or horseshoe style.

Practice 5, page 31
1. letting; showing 2. to win; to contact 3. to make 4. introducing; giving 5. making

Letter Practice 1, page 32
1. selected 2. discussions 3. place
4. In addition 5. as well as 6. attached
7. contact 8. deciding

Letter Practice 2, page 33
1. Mr. (period) 2. confirm
3. conference 4. indicated 5. reserve
6. said 7. at 8. (period) 9. cost projection 10. choosing

Letter Practice 3, page 34
Letters will vary but must follow the model letter format.

UNIT 5, page 35

Getting Started, page 35
1. 50,000 2. 100,000 3. 25,000
4. 100,000 5. 315,000 6. $36,000
7. $90,000 8. $90,000 9. 02/05
10. 03/05

Practice 1, page 37
1. a and b are appropriate in style and content; c is inappropriate. "Would" is more polite than "could"; "some chip sets" should be replaced with the exact number of sets required.
2. a and c are appropriate in style and content; b would not be asked. It is assumed that items are in stock.
3. b and c are appropriate in style and content; a is too informal. Try, "Please invoice us for the amount due and the method of payment required."
4. a and c are appropriate in style and content; b is threatening. It would not be used in a business letter.

Practice 2, page 38
1. Computer Chip Sets and Drives
2. 100,000 each of Intex 440SX, Ultra ATA/88, and Ardo 6L and 50,000 each of AGB 5/x/233 and Intex 600
3. Two weeks before assembly starts
4. Mr. Walter Granger 5. Ms. Marcia Collins 6. Upon receipt of invoice and components

Practice 3, page 38
1. with 2. for 3. of 4. on

Practice 4, page 39 *Answers will vary.*
2. We look forward to receiving the chip sets by Tuesday afternoon.
3. The components should be sent to our Receiving Department on or before the first of next week.
4. It is important that the goods be received before the middle of this summer.
5. The items must be on hand by the middle of next month.

Practice 5, page 39
2. As usual, we will pay upon goods received in satisfactory condition.
3. As we agreed, we will send a deposit of half the amount and pay the balance when the goods are delivered.
4. As we have done in the past, we will pay by credit card when we place the order.
5. As we discussed, we have enclosed a completed credit reference form.

Letter Practice 1, page 40
1. following 2. items 3. Delivery
4. enclosed 5. order 6. balance
7. submit 8. concerning

Letter Practice 2, page 41
1. Order 2. order 3. from 4. catalog. (period) 5. delivered 6. to 7. cost
8. If 9. at 10. yours, (comma)

Letter Practice 3, page 42
Letters will vary but must follow the model letter format.

UNIT 6, page 43

Getting Started, page 43
Dalway Computers and Tiger Industrials will be called.

Practice 1, page 45
1. b. Note: a is also appropriate in style and content; c is impolite. The verb "got" would not be used. Try, "We have received your order."
2. c. Note: b may be true, but it isn't an appropriate explanation. a is too blunt. Try, "Unfortunately, those items are currently out of stock."
3. c. Note: b is also appropriate in style and content. a may be true, but it is inappropriate in style. Try, "We'll notify you as soon as the item is shipped."
4. c. Note: a and b may be true, but they are not appropriate Closings.

Practice 2, page 46
The following subject lines contain specific information and should be checked: 2, 4, 5, and 7

Practice 3, page 46 *Answers will vary.*
2. Your furniture order of September 6 has been received and confirmed.

3. We have received your e-mail of August 10.
4. Thank you for your fax and purchase order of March 2.
5. Your order letter of January 9 arrived yesterday.

Practice 4, page 47 *Answers may vary.*
2. As I mentioned over the phone this morning, Intex chipsets are out of stock.
3. As I told you in our telephone conversation last week, all items on your purchase order are no longer in production.
4. In our meeting last Tuesday, I told you we are unable to fill your order at this time.

Practice 5, page 47
1. d 2. a 3. c 4. b

Letter Practice 1, page 48
1. fax 2. in stock 3. requested
4. ordered 5. additional 6. important
7. anything 8. number

Letter Practice 2, page 49
1. Ms. 2. received 3. for 4. has
5. at 6. than 7. are 8. for
9. solution 10. Sincerely

Letter Practice 3, page 50
Letters will vary but must follow the model letter format.

UNIT 7, page 51

Getting Started, page 51
1. Digital Camera (N) 2. XL-Lite (N)
3. Fall (E) 4. 270g (9.5oz) (W) 5. 2x optical zoom lens (W) 6. lithium battery, rechargeable battery, AC adapter (W, N) 7. 260 (N, E) 8. 80 (E)
9. ? 10. ? 11. ? 12. e-mail link (W)

Practice 1, page 53
1. **a** and **c** are appropriate in style and content; **b** is too informal. It's a statement used in conversations with friends.
2. **a** and **b** are appropriate in style and content; **c** may be true, but it is better to be humble.
3. **a** and **b** are appropriate in style and content; **c** is too general. Be specific about what you want sent.
4. **a** and **c** are appropriate in style and content; **b** is too informal. Try, "Would it be possible for you to forward the brochure as soon as possible?"

Practice 2, page 54
1. in 2. on 3. In 4. in 5. on 6. on

Practice 3, pages 54–55
2. S
3. F; Our main offices and its branches, which are located on every continent, can help your company promote its products.

4. F; Since 1959, we have been the major supplier of electronic equipment for hospitals.
5. S

Practice 4, page 55 *Answers will vary.*
2. Would you please give me your most current prices?
3. Please have your sales representative call me.
4. Would you please tell me when the product is available?
5. I would appreciate your faxing me a list of distributors.

Letter Practice 1, page 56
1. received 2. known 3. possible
4. reference 5. custom 6. appreciate
7. earliest 8. continued

Letter Practice 2, page 57
1. April 13, (comma) 2. Dear 3. in
4. April 5. are 6. us 7. interested
8. to 9. would 10. discuss

Letter Practice 3, page 58
Letters will vary but must follow the model letter format.

UNIT 8, page 59

Getting Started, page 59
1. Mar 19 / Mar 27
2. Information not given
3. Mar 20 / Mar 27
4. Mar 20 / Mar 27
5. Information not given
6. Information not given
7. Information not given
8. Information not given / Mar 20
9. Information not given / Mar 20
10. Information not given / Mar 20
11. Mar 18 / Mar 20
12. information not given
13. information not given
14. information not given
15. information not given
16. Mar 18 / Mar 23

Practice 1, page 61
1. **a** and **b** are appropriate in style and content; **c** may be true, but this statement would more likely be used in an advertisement than a letter.
2. **b** and **c** are appropriate in style and content; **a** is not a good sales technique. Try, "We will have a sales representative call you to discuss any concerns you might have."
3. **a** and **c** are appropriate in style and content; **b** could be appropriate if the rest of the letter matched this informal style.
4. **a** and **c** are appropriate in style and content; **b** is not a good sales technique. Try, "We will have a sales representative call you to discuss the features of our new camera."

Practice 2, page 62
2. (6); (60) 3. one hundred; (100); one; (1) 4. February 1st or January 2nd
5. fifteenth; fifth 6. four; 4; forty; 40

Practice 3, page 63
2. A sales representative will e-mail or telephone you.
3. We do not have the 999X camera, but we have a newer model.
4. We appreciate your order, and we look forward to working with you again.
5. The brochure is ready now, but the camera will be sent next week.

Practice 4, page 63
2. In addition, we are shipping the software this week.
3. In addition, I look forward to working with you in the future.
4. I am also attaching an order form.
5. In addition, I am enclosing information on our new video camera.

Letter Practice 1, page 64
1. your 2. pleased 3. addition
4. custom-made 5. separate 6. further
7. hesitate 8. inquiry

Letter Practice 2, page 65
1. Walland, (comma) 2. your 3. As
4. I am also 5. our 6. discuss 7. of
8. forward 9. be 10. inquiry

Letter Practice 3, page 66
Letters will vary but must follow the model letter format.

UNIT 9, page 67

Getting Started, page 67
1. (1) word processing software
2. 5/6 3. (1) BookBest 4. (2) GolfBest
5. bookcase 6. bookcase without shelves 7. information not given

Practice 1, page 69
1. **a** and **b** are appropriate in style and content; **c** may be true, but should not be in the Opening.
2. **a** and **c** are appropriate in style and content; **b** is sarcastic. Thank people for something you are genuinely thankful for. Try, "Thank you for your attention to this matter."
3. **a** and **b** are appropriate in style and content; **c** is insulting.
4. **b** and **c** are appropriate in style and content; **a** is too threatening. It would never be used in a formal letter.

Practice 2, page 70

Contraction	Formal
2. we're	we are
3. can't	cannot
4. wasn't	was not
5. isn't	is not

Practice 3, pages 70-71
2. The package was poorly wrapped.
3. The items were loosely packed.
4. The goods were insufficiently insured.
5. The invoice was incorrectly added.

Practice 4, page 71
2. Four packages — all from NewMedia Publishers — were sent to the wrong address.
3. The final order form — the one with so many changes — was difficult to read.
4. The entire contents of the shipment — bookcases, chairs, and desks — were damaged.
5. All of the supplies — the books, paper, tape, and disks — were lost in transit.

Letter Practice 1, page 72
1. order 2. incorrect 3. returning
4. cover 5. missing 6. correct
7. invoice 8. receiving

Letter Practice 2, page 73
1. disappointed 2. were 3. shipment
4. take back 5. ten 6. received 7. our
8. quickly 9. and 10. for

Letter Practice 3, page 74
Letters will vary but must follow the model letter format.

UNIT 10, page 75

Getting Started, page 75
1. Virtual Plan 2. damaged CD-ROM
3. outdated tracking software
4. damaged CD-ROM 5. sent new versions with 10% discount coupon
6. sent replacement CD-ROM with a complimentary training video 7. sent replacement CD-ROM with a complimentary training video

Practice 1, page 77
1. **a** and **b** are appropriate in style and content; **c** is OK, but a more formal sentence would be more appropriate. Try, "We apologize that our latest catalogs are out of stock."
2. **b** and **c** are appropriate in style and content; **a** is too sarcastic. Try, "In the future, we will use a more reliable delivery courier."
3. **b** and **c** are appropriate in style and content; **a** would never be used. A customer would never be sent to a competitor. Try, "Even though we don't have precisely the item you are looking for you, we have alternatives that will fit your needs."
4. **b** and **c** are appropriate in style and content; **a** is too sarcastic. Try, "In the future, we will make every effort to make sure your shipment arrives in the same condition as it left our factory."

Practice 2, page 78
2. replacement 3. credit 4. refund
5. replacement 6. replacement

Practice 3, page 79
2. apology 3. action 4. action
5. apology 6. action

Practice 4, page 79 *Answers may vary.*
2. Three (3) CDs were replaced.
3. We have sent 12 accounting packages to your attention.
4. Your account will be credited $1000.
5. Two manuals have been sent under separate cover.
6. You will be given $80 as a store credit.

Letter Practice 1, page 80
1. regarding 2. apologize
3. inconvenience 4. replacement
5. enclosing 6. regret 7. damaged
8. providing

Letter Practice 2, page 81
1. May 16, (**comma**) 2. Replace **receiving** with **received** 3. replace (**12**) with (**2**) 4. Change **incorrectly were sent** to **were sent incorrectly** 5. Spell out **1** (**one**) 6. Replace **request** with **requested** 7. Replace **compliments** with **complimentary** 8. Replace **inconveniencing** with **inconvenienced** 9. Replace **or** with **and** 10. Sincerely yours, (**comma**)

Letter Practice 3, page 82
Letters will vary but must follow the model letter format.

UNIT 11, page 83

Getting Started, page 83
1. Jun 30 2. n/a 3. ? 4. ? 5. ? 6. ?
7. ? 8. Jul. 15 9. Aug. 18 10. n/a
11. n/a 12. n/a 13. ? 14. Jun. 30, Jul. 15 15. ? 16. Jul. 31 17. ? 18. ?
19. n/a 20. n/a 21. Jul. 4 22. n/a

Practice 1, page 85
1. **a** and **b** are appropriate in style and content; **c** may be true, but it is impolite. Try, "Payment was due on the 31st."
2. **a** and **c** are appropriate in style and content; **b** is too sarcastic. Try, "If there is a reason you have been unable to pay, please contact us to arrange a different payment schedule."
3. **a** and **b** are appropriate in style and content; **c** is not true. A customer's financial difficulties are a company's problem. The goal is to get paid. Try, "If there is a reason you have been unable to pay, please contact us to arrange a different payment schedule."
4. **a** and **c** are appropriate in style and content; **b** is OK, but is threatening. This sentence would be used in the second or third collection letter sent.

Practice 2, page 86
1. by 2. no later than 3. within 4. on
5. by 6. on

Practice 3, page 86
1. the 2. The 3. the 4. an 5. the 6. a

Practice 4, page 87
2. I look forward to hearing from you about this issue.
3. Singalay looks forward to serving you in the future.
4. I look forward to discussing a payment plan that will work for both of us.
5. We look forward to continuing our relationship with Gornan Industries.
6. I look forward to knowing your thoughts on this topic.
7. I look forward to working with you again.

Letter Practice 1, page 88
1. balance 2. invoice 3. due 4. in full
5. reminder 6. payment 7. credit
8. Accountant

Letter Practice 2, page 89
1. Replace **A** balance with **The** balance
2. Replace **within** June 30 with **on** or **by** June 30 3. Replace **dues** with **due**
4. Replace **a** fifth with **the** fifth 5. Replace **receiving** with **received** 6. Replace **the** collection agency with **a** collection agency 7. Replace **on** the end of the month with **by** the end of the month 8. Replace **the** valued client with **a** valued client 9. Replace **settle** with **settling** 10. Replace **Goodbye** with **Sincerely yours,** or **Sincerely,**

Letter Practice 3, page 90
Letters will vary but must follow the model letter format.

UNIT 12, page 91

Getting Started, page 91
1. $5,677.34 2. 8/30 3. 778-721
4. 8/30 5. 8/30 6. Callatar 7. wait

Practice 1, page 93
1. **b** and **c** are appropriate in style and content; **a** is too angry. Try, "According to our records, we have satisfied our financial obligation to your company."
2. **a** and **b** are appropriate in style and content; **c** is appropriate in style, but not in content for the Focus of a letter. It should be in the Closing.
3. **b** and **c** are appropriate in style and content; **a** is appropriate in style, but not content for the Closing of a letter. It should be the Focus.

Practice 2, page 94
1. already 2. already 3. still 4. already
5. yet 6. yet 7. still

Practice 3, page 95
1. August 31, 20— 2. 3 July 20—
3. 14 March 20— 4. July 17
5. December 1, 20—

Practice 4, page 95
2. According to our records, we have already made this payment.
3. Given the misunderstanding, we think it would be fair for you to offer us a discount.
4. Considering the weather problems, I understand why your payment was late.
5. After reviewing your letter, I'd like to discuss the original costs with you.
6. If you have any questions, please do not hesitate to contact me.

Practice 5, page 95
2. Thank you for reminding us to pay.
3. Thank you for your understanding about our late payment.
4. Thank you, in advance, for giving us an extension on this payment.
5. I want to thank you personally for your patience while we were moving offices.

Letter Practice 1, page 96
1. policy 2. accounts 3. issued
4. check 5. stop 6. authorization
7. installments 8. track

Letter Practice 2, page 97
1. Replace **remind** with **reminder**
2. Replace **not received the original invoice still** with **still not received the original invoice** or **not received the original invoice yet**.
3. reminder, (**comma**)
4. Replace **December, 12** with **December 12**
5. purposes, (**comma**)
6. Replace **very would be** with **would be very**
7. Replace **invoice** with **invoices**
8. Replace **you can already** send with **you can still** send
9. Replace **December 31,** with **December 31**
10. Replace **attend** with **attention**

Letter Practice 3, page 98
Letters will vary but must follow the model letter format.

UNIT 13, page 99
Getting Started, page 99
Lee Ming-Tang: Introduction (✔)
Michelle Fung: Announcement (To do)
Matsuo Yukiko: Reference (✔)
Luis Martinez: Reference (To do)
Kay Jens: Announcement (To do)

Practice 1, page 101
1. Ms. Matsuo was a summer intern at Bozeman International from May to August this year. As an intern, Ms. Matsuo was responsible for assisting our professional staff with their duties. She was efficient, punctual, and detail-oriented. She worked well under pressure and got along well with the staff.
2. I recommend Ms. Matsuo for any position that requires a self-starter who is able to follow through on a task.
3. Please do not hesitate to contact me if you have any questions.

Practice 2, page 101
1. F 2. O 3. A 4. F 5. A 6. A
7. O 8. A

Practice 3, page 102
1. professionally 2. efficient
3. accurately 4. attractive 5. effectively
6. complete 7. highly 8. honest
9. happy 10. full

Practice 4, page 103
1. We are pleased to announce that Michelle Fung has joined our firm as senior account specialist.
2. She will be calling on you in the next few weeks to introduce herself and discuss any questions you have about your orders.
3. Let's all extend a friendly welcome to Michelle Fung.

Practice 5, page 104
1. b 2. a 3. a 4. a 5. b

Practice 6, page 104
1. has served 2. participated
3. worked 4. has designed 5. won

Practice 7, page 106
1. This letter will introduce Lee Ming-Tang, our sales manager who will be in your city October 12 – 14 scouting out new leads.
2. Mr. Lee has been with our company for ten years and has rapidly moved up from a regional sales position to manager of our sales division . . .
3. Thank you in advance for meeting with Ming-Tang.

Practice 8, page 106
1. a 2. b 3. a 4. a 5. a 6. a

Practice 9, page 107
2. He not only designed the new product but also designed the marketing slogan.
3. Allen is not only a fair manager but also a caring one.
4. She not only works harder than anyone I've ever met but also plays golf with complete devotion.
5. He would like not only to tour your main offices but also to see your production facility.

6. You not only will enjoy meeting each other but also will have a lot in common.

Letter Practice, page 108
Letters will vary but must follow the model letter format.

UNIT 14, page 109
Getting Started, page 109
1. Jan. 5 2. Jan. 5 3. Jan. 5 4. Jan. 5
5. Jan. 5 6. Jan. 3 7. Jan. 3 8. Jan. 3
9. Jan. 3 10. Jan. 3 11. Jan. 6 12. Jan. 7
13. Jan. 7 14. Jan. 8 15. Jan. 8 16. Jan. 10
17. Jan. 10 18. Jan. 10 19. Jan. 11
20. Jan. 10

Practice 1, page 111
1. All accounts previously handled through Kuala Lumpur will now be managed through our new office in Singapore . . .
2. Your new account manager, Siling Wu, will contact you shortly to introduce herself and to answer any questions you might have.
3. We look forward to working with you from our new office.

Practice 2, page 111
2. Which two offices are closing?
3. Who will call?
4. Where is the office moving?
5. When is the telephone number going to change?

Practice 3, page 112
2. I will call you (in a few weeks) to discuss your concerns.
3. You will receive an e-mail (tomorrow) from our new branch manager.
4. Customers will receive an invitation to visit our new offices (soon).
5. We will send our new office directory so it will arrive (before the end of the year).

Practice 4, page 113
1. Our annual New Year's Promotion begins today!
2. Go to http://www.electronix.com/product/promotion/htm for more information, or call us at 1-888-555-5353
3. As a Gold card customer, you are important to us, and we want to reward you for your loyalty . . .

Practice 5, page 114
1. b 2. a 3. a 4. a 5. b

Practice 6, page 114
1. b 2. a 3. a 4. b

Practice 7, page 116
1. We are recalling the Photophone 642, which was shipped to you on December 5.